Step-Parenting Without the Drama

THE ART OF
Stepping *Back*

FOR EVERY STEPPARENT WHO FEELS STUCK,
UNSEEN, OR JUST PLAIN EXHAUSTED

Mary Dixon

Step-Parenting without the Drama
By
Mary Dixon

This is a work of creative nonfiction. Some parts have been fictionalized in varying degrees for various purposes.

Copyright © Mary Dixon, 2025

All rights reserved. No part of this book may be reproduced in any form by any electronic or mechanical means, including information storage and retrieval systems, without permission in writing from the publisher, except by a reviewer who may quote brief passages in a review.

DISCLAIMER

This book is intended to educate and inform. It is not intended to replace professional advice, counseling, or therapy. The author has drawn on their own experiences, research, and conversations with other stepfamilies to write this book; however, it should not be considered professional psychological, legal, or medical advice. Every family is different, and what works for one may not work for another. Readers are encouraged to apply common sense, seek professional help as needed, and adapt any of the tactics shown here to suit their own needs and ideals. The ideas discussed, especially those related to Nacho Parenting, are intended to help people establish boundaries, improve their emotional well-being, and foster healthier relationships with their stepfamilies. They are not meant to weaken parental authority or cause problems in families; instead, they equip stepparents with the skills to protect themselves and stay connected. The author and publisher are not responsible for any results that occur from following the ideas or suggestions in this book. If you use this material, you agree to these terms.

TABLE OF CONTENTS

Disclaimer	3
Preface	6
Introduction	8

Chapter 1
Nacho Kids, Nacho Problem — 14

Chapter 2
You're Not Their Parent — 34

Chapter 3
When You Try Too Hard You Lose Yourself — 54

Chapter 4
Let the Bio Parents Handle It — 72

Chapter 5
You're Not the Household Manager — 94

Chapter 6
Don't Discipline - That's Not Your Lane — 116

Chapter 7
Power of Presence Without Pressure — 134

Chapter 8
Boundaries Aren't Barriers They're Lifelines   148

Chapter 9
You Matter Too Reclaiming Your Identity   158

Chapter 10
Talk to Your Partner Not Their Kids   166

Chapter 11
Protect Your Relationship First   176

Chapter 12
You're Not Cold   You're Clear   184

Conclusion
Loving Smart, Living Peacefully   192

PREFACE

Being a stepparent is one of the most demanding roles a person can undertake. You may feel like you need to love unconditionally, serve silently, and give up things without getting anything in return, often for kids you didn't raise, rules you didn't make, and obligations you never agreed to. It is a job that is full of love, hope, anger, and sometimes severe emotional exhaustion. If you feel like this' this book is for you, the stepparent who feels like they have to do everything, wonders where they fit in the family, and wonders if there's a way to show up without getting overwhelmed by all the emotions. Step-Parenting without the Drama: The Art of Stepping Back doesn't mean not becoming involved. It's about changing how we think about engagement. It's about giving yourself permission to take a step back, breathe, make room, and get your calm back without feeling bad about it. You won't simply find strategies here; you'll also find clarity. A way to show up with love while still respecting your limits. A reminder that you can be there without doing too much.

And most importantly, you're not alone. You are important. What you do is essential. And your serenity is necessary, this book is your chance to love better and live more freely in a role that was never supposed to cost you.

INTRODUCTION

Blended families don't come with a perfect, one-size-fits-all instruction manual. No one tells you about the emotional landmines, the invisible work, or the continual second- guessing. You enter a situation that is already in motion, with norms, habits, and loyalties already in place. And yet, somehow, you have to "fit in," help out, get along, and keep the peace without stepping on anyone's toes. You never officially signed up for this job, yet here you are, trying your best. This is where Nacho Parenting comes in—not as an act of rebellion, and not as a way to avoid responsibility, but as a healthy approach built on the understanding that certain responsibilities were never yours to begin with— helping you protect your sanity, your relationship, and your sense of self. This is what Nacho Parenting is all about:

> "These are nacho kids; it's not your job to raise, discipline, or fix them."

That doesn't mean you don't care, and it doesn't mean you shouldn't be present in their lives. It only means you need to step back, let the biological parents take the lead, and stop attempting to do something that was never yours to do.

Your permission to let go and breathe again

If you're the kind of person who instinctively wants to help and solve problems, the thought of standing back can be complex to take in at first. You may have stepped into this family hoping to help, connect, and make life a little easier for everyone. You might have believed that if you just gave enough of yourself—by cooking meals, helping with homework, and showing up to every event—you would be embraced as part of the family. But if you're reading this, you probably already know the unpleasant truth: in stepfamilies, doing more does not mean being more appreciated. Sometimes, the more you give, the more invisible—or even disliked— you can end up feeling. And that tiredness and feeling like no one sees you isn't your fault. It's a sign that you're trying to be a parent in a place where you don't have power, a history, or a stable emotional base. This book gives you the go-ahead to stop working so hard. To stop doing too much, stop being a parent when you don't have to, and get back your energy, identity, and calm. Affection isn't something you have to work for by doing things for others. You don't have to reprimand kids who aren't ready to listen to what you have to say. This is your home —you shouldn't have to sacrifice your well-being to prove you belong. You need to breathe again. The first step is to step back from the turmoil and reconnect with yourself.

You're Not Their Parent—You're the Peacekeeper

One of the most critical changes in your mind when you start Nacho Parenting is this: you are not their parent. That's not a bad thing. It's a limit. And it's an important one. You are not here to take the place of a biological parent. You don't have to teach life lessons, discipline, change attitudes, or enforce rules. That's the lane for biological parents. When there is a disagreement, you don't talk to the kids; you talk to your partner alone. You don't demand behaviour when duties aren't done; instead, let your partner deal with it. When someone is rude to you, you don't just deal with it; you leave with dignity and emotional maturity. This isn't being weak. This is power. You are not the enforcer; you are the "emotional anchor." The safe space, not the person in charge. The one who maintains calm even when the storm is raging. By doing this, you not only safeguard your mental and emotional health but also your relationship with your partner and your stepchildren. Here's the truth: when stepchildren don't perceive you as their parent—and most don't—any attempt to parent them might feel like a threat. It makes everything tense. It causes fights for power. It breaks bonds. But what if you take a step back and focus on being kind, impartial, consistent, and respectful? That's when trust starts to grow. Slowly, silently, and naturally.

Stepping Back Is Survival, Not Being Selfish

To be clear, Nacho Parenting does not mean giving up on the family dynamic. It's not a reason to stop caring or check out. It's about living in a system that wasn't designed for you to excel in without limitations. Yes, blended families are full of love, but they are also quite complicated. Step-parents often feel overwhelmed by their emotions when there are unclear responsibilities and expectations. The guilt keeps coming. The anger grows. Your relationship with partner becomes strained. You forget who you were before all of this happened, since your own needs are always at the bottom of the list. Nacho Parenting is the life jacket. It helps you remain afloat, breathe, and keep your emotions in check while everyone else finds out their dynamic. It gives responsibility back to the biological parents, where it belongs. And it lets you care from a place of clarity, not control. You are still a part of the family, but only on your terms. You are still there, but not too much. You still care, but you stop lugging things that aren't yours. That's not being selfish. That will last.

A Better Way to Go

This book isn't about giving up or walking away. It's a roadmap to realign—helping you remember what your role is and what it isn't. To "set limits without burning bridges" and "find joy in your home again"—not by controlling the kids, but by getting your peace back. We're going to discuss:

- Why it's not your business to discipline
- How to avoid performing all the chores around the house; what to do when you feel mistreated or unnoticed;
- How to talk to your partner in a way that works behind closed doors
- How to stay involved without forcing connections
- How to take care of your emotional and mental health without feeling bad

You will learn how to "step back without stepping away." You'll look at real-life examples, scripts, mindset changes, and practical limits that work in the messy, unpredictable reality of being a step-parent. And most importantly, you'll remember that you're not alone. Thousands of stepparents have been where you are—feeling exhausted and overwhelmed—but many have found peace by choosing the Nacho route. It's not always simple, but it is possible. And it begins right now, with this first brave step back. Let's walk this path together.

CHAPTER 1
Nacho Kids, Nacho Problem

A radical mindset shift that changes everything.

What Nacho Parenting Means

Joining a blended family can feel overwhelming. You might have felt pushed to "blend" in ways that don't quite fit who you are—expected to treat the kids like your own, be deeply involved, care passionately, and above all, tiptoe around everyone's feelings. That mix is hard to understand, and it's where many stepparents give up. Nacho Parenting is different. Something that gives you room. Something that says, "You can love this family without losing yourself in it." And that starts with realizing a basic, straightforward fact: These kids are not your biological children; they are "nacho" kids. You didn't bring them up. You didn't make the rules that made them who they are. You don't have to fix, discipline, or manage them. Being a Nacho parent isn't about being indifferent or disconnected. It's about clearly knowing the difference between caring and carrying. Caring means showing support and love without taking on burdens that aren't yours. Carrying means shouldering responsibilities that were never meant for you—and refusing to do that is how you protect your sanity and your relationships.

Giving Up a Role That Isn't Realistic

Many stepparents begin with good intentions. You want to be welcomed, helpful, and involved. You drive people around, cook for them, make sure they go to bed on time, and keep an eye on their screen time—all to be present. But when your efforts are ignored or met with coldness, it's easy to feel unappreciated, start resenting the situation, and believe you're failing.

What is the truth?
It's not your fault. It's an unrealistic expectation. Mixed families often have existing loyalties and emotional scars. Kids may still be getting used to their parents' divorce, remarriage, different homes, or even the fact that they are still loyal to each other. When a stepparent assumes a parental role, even if they mean well, it can make the child feel confused, defensive, or distrustful, and it can leave the adult feeling frustrated and tired. Nacho Parenting alleviates stress by declaring, "You don't have to be a parent to be valuable." You can step back, change your role, and show up in a way that doesn't wear you out emotionally.

Help Without Giving Up

What does Nacho Parenting look like in real life? You don't deal with discipline. If a kid talks back, won't do their duties, or breaks a rule, don't speak to them. You step back and let your partner, the biological parent, deal with it. You don't micromanage behavior. You cease keeping an eye on everything. You stop trying to "fix" the dynamic, which is tiring. You don't push yourself too hard. You don't have to plan drop-offs, set up appointments, cook dinner every night, or make sure homework is done. You stop giving more than you get. You still care, though. It shows you care with clarity. You're helping by being there, staying calm, and being kind, not by controlling or forcing authority. You let the biological parents raise the kids. You stay in your lane, and that's where peace starts.

Why This Change Will Save Your Relationships and Your Mind

When you try to do everything in a mixed family, such as help, enforce rules, and hold everyone together emotionally, you often wind up feeling overworked, ignored, and stressed. Resentment grows. Your relationship with your partner gets worse. Your self-assurance goes down. You feel like no matter what you do, it will never be enough. It's not about stepping away when you're a nacho parent. It's about walking smartly. It helps you avoid burnout, and it typically also protects the relationship. You can begin to heal emotionally when you stop trying to control things that aren't yours to control. You don't react to every fight anymore. You're no longer stuck in problems that weren't yours to fix. You begin to respond instead of react, help instead of control, and truly live instead of just getting by. This change benefits everyone—not just you. The kids feel less pressure.

Biological parents feel stronger. And you? You can finally show up as your whole self, not just a stressed-out version.

Being a Nacho parent isn't just a trend; it's a way of thinking. One that is based on "boundaries, clarity, and emotional self-protection." You won't have to give up your peace of mind to raise someone else's children in a system where you lack the power, experience, or support to do well. In the following chapters, we'll discuss how to apply this way of thinking in everyday life, including how to address problems, build trust, manage expectations, and maintain a safe relationship. For now, know this:

- You aren't giving up.
- You're becoming smarter.

You're picking a route that works for everyone, not just the kids or your partner, but also for you.

Why You Don't Owe Anyone a Parental Role

When you become a stepparent, there is frequently a silent but strong demand to "step up"—to take on parenting duties, cover emotional gaps, and show your worth via hard work. It can be tiring and quite unfair to feel like you have to meet an expectation, whether your partner says it out loud, the situation suggests it, or you feel it inside. But here's the fact that needs to be expressed out loud:

You don't have to take on the parenting role for others' children, be your partner's caretaker, or run the entire household.

Being in a relationship doesn't mean you're obligated to take on certain roles, now or ever.

If you fall in love with someone who has kids, your heart may naturally open up to the children. You might wish to help. You might want to connect. You might even be delighted to be a part of their life. But just because you love your partner doesn't mean you have to become a co- parent. You didn't make these kids. You weren't there for the first several years of their lives. You didn't make the rules, rituals, or emotional foundations that kids live by. You don't have to be the disciplinarian, household manager, or emotional fixer simply because you live together or are in a relationship. Trying to do so typically makes things worse, rather than better. It can create tension between you and the kids, put a strain on your relationship with your partner, and leave you emotionally exhausted. Nacho Parenting is a more effective way to stay involved without getting too stressed.

To be a good parent, you need more than just being close.

Being around kids is not the same as being responsible for them. To be a good parent, you need to be there and have authority. But in most blended families, stepparents don't have that authority. They have to follow the rules, but they can't make them. They are requested to help, but people don't always respect them. That imbalance exacerbates the situation for everyone. In the meantime, the kids may feel confused, defensive, or angry, especially if they think you're trying to take the position of a biological parent. Nacho Parenting helps alleviate this tension and reduce stress. It lets you step back from the role you were never really meant to have and instead focus on being "a kind, stable adult in the room"—someone who supports the system without trying to control it.

Letting Go of Guilt and Expectation

Many stepparents feel guilty. Feeling guilty for not accomplishing enough, feeling bad for desiring space, and feeling bad for not connecting with the kids right away. That guilt can make you do too much, work too hard, and make too many promises that you can't keep. Feeling guilty doesn't mean you're obligated to act or fix things that aren't your responsibility. It's okay to love your partner sincerely, support the family structure, and still set clear limits on your emotional energy. You don't have to feel bad if you don't go to every game, pack every lunch, or make sure every consequence is carried out. That is the job of the biological parents, not yours. You aren't failing if you stop being a "parent." It means you're choosing a better method to be there that respects your abilities and clarifies your position.

What You Offer Still Matters, Even If It's Different

Not wanting to be a parent doesn't mean you go away. It means you provide in a new way. You don't make the rules or enforce them; instead, you are the quiet presence. The grown-up who listens without making a judgment. The one who doesn't ask for loyalty or obedience but slowly gains trust over time. Children, especially those in blended families, need adults who are trustworthy, dependable, and emotionally stable. They don't always require another person in charge. Sometimes they need someone who respects their space, stays calm, and doesn't try to dominate them. Letting go of the pressure to be a parent allows you to build real, authentic connections with the kids. You may have fun together without any stress. You can love someone without taking on a role that isn't yours. And it, which may come as a surprise, typically leads to deeper trust and stronger bonds over time. You don't have to be a parent to anyone. You owe it to yourself to be honest and to respect your emotional limits. Being a Nacho parent doesn't mean giving up; it means finding new ways to help your family without losing your peace. You're not resigning by walking out of the parent position. You are just choosing to interact in a way that is healthy, long-lasting, and respectful for everyone, including you. We'll discuss why attempting to offer too much, even with good intentions, often leads to burnout, resentment, and emotional exhaustion in the next section. And more crucially, how to change that pattern for good.

You Didn't Create the Chaos

When you became a part of your partner's life, you probably entered into a family system that was already in motion, with its history, rhythms, routines, and emotional baggage. You came in as an outsider, yet you might have immediately felt like you had to fix everything that was broken. And even if you didn't break everything, you might still be striving to keep it all together. But every stepparent needs to hear and believe this:

> You are not to blame for the family's problems. You don't have to clean it up.

The ex-partners' anger, the kids' bad behavior, the lack of communication, and the emotional scars that haven't healed yet—all of it started before you. And you alone won't be able to fix any of it.

You Entered a Story That Was Already There

Stepping into a new family and building a fresh dynamic isn't easy, particularly after significant changes such as divorce, separation, or losing a parent. You are entering a story that already has layers, trauma, and implicit expectations as you come into that space. That tale is not yours. You are a supporting character, and sometimes you watch. However, too frequently, stepparents feel like they have to be the ones who keep things stable. You may have to be the go-between when people talk to each other, the one who keeps things calm during conflicts, or the one who fixes things when they break. You might do things that no one asked you to do, like plan schedules, take care of logistics, or correct bad behavior, because you think it's the right thing to do. However, in real life, these actions are often overlooked or met with resistance. Why? Because you are trying to mend situations that aren't your fault. You are trying to change the finish of a movie that you have never seen the beginning of. You can't do that, and it will only make you angry, frustrated, and emotionally drained.

Letting Go Is a Form of Emotional Wisdom

Knowing what you can't handle isn't avoiding it; it's being emotionally intelligent. You know that just because you're there doesn't mean you have to take care of everyone's feelings, choices, or actions. If a youngster is disrespectful or ignores you, it's not your responsibility to address the issue. It's not your business to step in when your spouse and their ex can't get along when they're parenting together. You can choose not to get involved in the emotional turmoil when the house is chaotic, tense, or split. That doesn't imply you don't care. You are choosing to respond instead of react, witness instead of absorb, and support your partner without trying to parent their children. That is power. That is smart. That's how you keep your peace.

Families That Are Healthy Need Responsibility, Not Martyrs

One of the biggest challenges for a stepparent is feeling like you have to do all the work, including cleaning, disciplining, and dealing with emotions, while the biological parents do nothing. This imbalance often makes people resentful without them having to say a word, especially when they don't care or fight back. But stepping in for everyone else doesn't fix the problem. It hides it. Not overcompensation, but accountability, is what makes families healthy. The biological parent should be the one to teach, correct, and lead their kids. No matter how damaged the co-parenting relationship is, they still have to deal with it. When you step in too often, you are letting your partner the bio parent away with not taking on their responsibilities. And by doing that, you take away their chance to grow, fix things, or lead. Taking a step back doesn't imply leaving the house. It means letting other people take charge, even if they don't do it the way you would. You don't have to raise someone else's kids or deal with the problems in their family's past. Your role is to live your truth with compassion, boundaries, and clarity.

You Should Have Peace in Your Own Home

Stepparents often feel like strangers in their own homes, having to tiptoe around problems, mediate fights, and try to make everyone get along. However, people usually overlook the fact that you also have the right to peace in your own home. You are not a visitor. You are a part of the team. You are a person with wants, restrictions, and feelings. Taking on everyone's emotional problems and trying to fix them doesn't bring people closer together. It makes you tired. It takes away your sense of self. You can start to regain your energy by letting go of the difficulties that were present before and not taking responsibility for things you didn't do. You stop creating chaos around you and start building a calm life within it. You don't have to put your health and happiness on the line to make other people feel better. That isn't selfish. That is balance. You didn't make the broken institutions, the disconnection, or the bad parenting that came before you. You don't have to fix things that were broken long before you got there. You are a gift to this family, not a cleaning crew. From now on, your job is to safeguard your peace, stick to your limits, and let the biological parents take care of their duties.

Parenting ≠ Peacekeeping

In many blended families, the stepparent is often the one who attempts to maintain peace, make everyone happy, and cope with the stress of living in a family that is always on edge. At first, it could seem like a good thing to do. After all, it seems like keeping the peace will keep the family together. However, that job can become tiring after a while. And even more significantly, it becomes lost. Being a parent and being a peacekeeper are not the same thing. Trying to do both as a stepparent might make you emotionally drained and cause your boundaries to break.

Stepparents Are Often the Emotional Middlemen

Many stepparents don't even realize that they are taking care of emotional issues that weren't theirs to deal with. When problems with co-parenting arise, you may need to help calm your partner down. You may step in when a child is acting out or not listening. You may even say that you are the one who keeps the family together by being patient, making sacrifices, and finding a middle ground. At first, this might seem helpful. But what starts as help can quickly become a full-time emotional job that no one asked you to undertake and that few people appreciate. In this case, the stepparent is the one who tries to maintain peace by preventing things from getting worse or emotions from escalating. But here's the hard truth: that's not your job. And doing this makes it harder for the biological parents to take charge of their duties.

Your health should not suffer for the sake of harmony.

Many stepparents feel that they must "make it work" by being flexible, forgiving, and patient at all times. But if you always give up your comfort to prevent fights or damaged feelings, you start to lose yourself. To avoid disagreement, you could begin to ignore your demands. You don't say anything when someone is rude to you. You let people break the rules around you to "keep things light." And all the while, you're steadily losing touch with your emotional limits. It's not right to try to keep the peace at the cost of your peace. It's not taking care of yourself. And over time, it builds up bitterness that quietly seeps into your relationship and your family. From the surface, it appears to be cooperation, but on the inside, it's suppression. One individual giving in all the time doesn't bring peace to a family. It comes from having clear duties, talking honestly, and being responsible together.

Healthy Boundaries Build Lasting Peace

One of the biggest mistakes people make when they are step-parents is thinking that disengaging equals giving up. That is not true. Taking a step back from a fight, letting your partner raise their kids, and not getting involved in every quarrel are not symptoms of failure. They indicate that things are improving. You don't have to worry about keeping the peace. You didn't make the family dynamic, so you don't have to change it. You don't have to be the one to explain, arbitrate, calm down, and settle every problem that comes up between other people. You need some room. Space to breathe emotionally. You have my permission to say, "That's not my problem." And the ability to let individuals deal with the inevitable repercussions of their actions without getting in the way. When you stick to those rules in a calm, compassionate, and consistent way, the whole house changes. People no longer regard you as someone who wants to dominate the situation. People perceive you as a stable and respectable person who allows others to take the lead. That's the kind of tranquilly that stays. Not the sort you have to work hard to keep, but the kind that comes from being clear and consistent.

Being Present Doesn't Mean You Have to Fix Everything

You can be busy without feeling stressed. You can care a lot about your home and your relationships without being the one who fixes every crack. Even if you're not always fixing every problem or making every awkward time better, your presence in the home is still significant. When you quit attempting to control the emotional climate, people have the freedom to take care of themselves. Instead of depending on you, your partner learns to respond. The kids start to think of their parents as the people who know what to do and how to do it. And most significantly, you are no longer working while burned out. In the classic sense, peacekeeping keeps you on the defensive. Instead, Nacho Parenting wants you to be responsive: calm, firm, and focused on your mental health. People frequently say that parenting, especially in a stepfamily, is like a service: the more you provide, the more valued you become. But the truth is that the more you strive to hold things together, the more likely you are to break. You are not there to cure problems, hide pain, or deal with chaos. Your job is to set limits, love with your whole heart, and protect your energy. That's not leaving. That's becoming clear.

CHAPTER 2
You're Not Their Parent

You're not replacing anyone — you're protecting yourself.

Letting Go of the "Fixer" Role

Many stepparents enter their roles with open hearts and good intentions. You might wish to put some order to the chaos, smooth out the rough spots, and relieve the stress in your new home. That instinct is OK. Wanting to help, make things stable, or support your partner shows that you are emotionally mature. But when that urge morphs into an unconscious promise to "fix" everything, it quickly becomes bad for you. Over time, managing everyone's concerns that no one can see can cause tension, anger, and exhaustion. You start to feel more like a referee or therapist than a partner, and often, people still don't appreciate or respect you for it. Letting go of the "fixer" identity doesn't mean leaving the people you love behind. It's about letting go of the idea that you have to address their problems.

You Don't Have to Fix Every Problem

There are often emotional struggles in blended families, including when co-parenting problems aren't worked out, rules aren't always the same, and there are communication gaps. If you're the kind of person who automatically sees what's wrong, you might feel that you have to be the one to fix everything. You make plans, help people deal with their feelings, remind them of things they need to do, stop fights, and strive to make everyone happy. Initially, you may feel helpful. However, after a while, that usefulness gives way to fatigue. You start to feel that you're working harder to keep the family together than the ones who have been there longer. It is crucial to remember that: You are not the basis of this family. You weren't there when it was built, and you don't have to keep it together. Your support can be helpful, but it should never hurt your mental health.

Helping Doesn't Mean Going Too Far

There is a fine line between being helpful and overstepping. Often, the fixer's job crosses the boundary. You can find yourself acting like a parent without even realizing it by correcting behavior, controlling routines, or trying to establish an instant connection through authority. It's easy to feel puzzled or upset when those efforts are met with resistance or apathy. The answer is simple: you're doing a job that no one asked you to do. Even if you mean well, kids and their biological parents sometimes regard the fixer as getting in the way. It's not about you; it's about the system. These positions were established long before you arrived. Trying to change them without complete authority will only cause problems. Nacho Parenting gives you a way out of this tiring loop. It allows you to help where you can, offer support from the sidelines, and relinquish any duties that weren't officially assigned to you.

You Should Be a Partner, Not a Project Manager

It's easy to want to fix things and forget that you're just one part of the family. You don't have to manage the house or handle all the emotions. You are someone's chosen partner, here to start a new life with them, not fix an old one. When you stop trying to control everything and focus on being present, the stress dissipates. You may enjoy your relationship without feeling like you have to do things all the time. You can care about the family without always feeling like you have to take action. You're not taking away love when you stop thinking like a fixer; you're bringing things back into balance.

Sustainable Help Has Limits

You don't have to stop assisting just because you're no longer the fixer. This means you help on purpose and within appropriate limitations. You stop working yourself into the ground trying to meet every need and start asking yourself:

- Is this my job?
- Did someone ask me to do something, or did I give it to myself?
- Will my participation assist, or will it make things even more complicated?

These questions help you know when to step back and when to get involved. They let you help without having to become a parent. They keep your emotional energy safe so you may stay present and not tired. You start fixing the one thing that matters—your peace—when you stop attempting to fix everyone else. You're not here to fix the problems that existed before you arrived. Your partner saw your worth just as you are—that's why this relationship began. And that's all it takes. That's all it takes. You can show up honestly, quietly, and sustainably if you stop thinking of yourself as a fixer. You don't have to rush to fix, plan, or organize every moving part anymore. You stand by what you believe. You make everything plain. You keep your peace. And by doing this, you give everyone, including yourself, room to grow in a better way.

Stepping Out of the Discipline Triangle

The "discipline triangle" is one of the most complex traps for stepparents to get into. In this unhealthy cycle, the stepparent becomes the enforcer, the child grows resistant, and the original parent either avoids responsibility or acts as a buffer. This triangle soon turns into a source of stress, anxiety, and emotional exhaustion for everyone concerned, especially the stepparent who never meant to be in that role in the first place. Realizing that you don't have to punish your partner's kids, and in many circumstances, shouldn't, is a strong and empowering thought. It lets you get out of a situation that usually does more harm than good and back to where you belong: as a helpful spouse, not as a behavior authority figure.

Discipline without Power Doesn't Work

Discipline needs more than just teaching or correcting; it requires trust, consistency, and an emotional connection. Over time, parents develop this foundation via shared experiences and a strong, natural bond. You probably don't have that bond with your stepchild yet, especially in the beginning. And without it, the child may feel like any attempt to discipline them is an invasion of privacy or even a betrayal. Kids can tell right away when an adult doesn't have the power to tell them what to do. They might push back, ignore you, or get angry, but not because they're being defiant. They want to defend their space and attachments. Even if you mean well, they may feel like you're going too far when you try to reprimand them. If you try to parent without the child's permission, it makes things tense. It makes you look like the "bad guy" Over time, this can make you feel distant instead of connected, and you may start to feel like the strict parent in a house where you want to be liked.

Letting the Biological Parent Take the Lead

In Nacho Parenting, the biological parent regains the power to discipline their child. They are the ones who made the rules, set the expectations, and made the relationship work. They also have the emotional power to change behavior in a way that works and lasts. Letting them take the lead doesn't mean you stop paying attention; it means keeping things clear at home. If your partner is the one who steps in when there is a disagreement or bad behavior, you can keep your relationship with the child safe. You don't become the reason for punishment or anger. You are always there for them, not someone who demands obedience, but someone who brings stability and peace. This is especially beneficial when a child is struggling with loyalty issues or unresolved feelings about their parents' divorce. If they regard you as a neutral, non-threatening adult, they are much more likely to talk to you over time, but only when they want to.

How to Stay Out of the "Good Cop, Bad Cop" Trap

The discipline triangle also has the hidden risk of the "good cop, bad cop" game. Even if your child doesn't want you to be involved, you can feel like you have to back up your partner's decisions or actions. Or worse, when your partner steps back, you have to enforce the rules, which means you have to deal with the emotional fallout on your own. This situation not only makes things harder between you and the child, but it also puts stress on your relationship. Over time, it may make you feel like you're doing all the emotional work of parenting without any support or backup. Getting out of this routine helps bring everything back into balance. Your partner is now in charge of the child's behavior. You're not the one giving out consequences anymore; you're helping the one who does. You don't have to explain, debate, or follow up. You can go back to being a kind adult instead of a strict one.

Redirecting Responsibility and Keeping the Peace

Nacho Parenting provides you with a precise script to follow when there is a behavior problem:

"This is something your mum or dad needs to deal with."

You don't have to yell, go over the rules, or correct the child personally. You leave in a calm, polite, and guilt-free way. If you're upset about anything that happened, it's best to discuss it with your partner privately, rather than in front of the child. You tell them you're worried, explain how it affects the home, and then let them deal with it as parents. This secret partnership prevents power struggles in public and maintains established boundaries. You can lower your stress, maintain a strong emotional connection with the child, and enhance communication with your partner by stepping outside of the discipline triangle. You stop worrying about things that aren't yours to address and instead focus on what you can control: your energy, your tone, and your presence. When you try to parent without authority, you often become tired and don't receive the thanks you deserve. Letting go of the desire to enforce discipline and allowing your partner to take the lead can help you avoid emotional burnout and stress in your relationship. You don't have discipline; the person who made the child, reared them, and is responsible for their emotional growth does. You have power when you step back, not when you move in.

Redefining What Love Looks Like

Love is one of the most complex aspects of blended families, especially for stepparents. People often say that if you love your stepchildren, you'll treat them like your own, get involved, and never hesitate to scold, guide, or discipline them. However, with a blended family, love takes on a different form. It's gentler, slower, and far more deliberate. To be a good stepparent, you need to shift your perspective on love in this role. It's not about being or doing everything. It's about being emotionally clear and having healthy boundaries when you show up. When you stop following the typical way of parenting and start thinking like a Nacho Parent, you realize that love doesn't have to be loud or all-consuming to be real.

Love Is Still Love Even When You Can't Control It

When you are a biological parent, love typically goes hand in hand with control, including setting rules, punishing bad behavior, and correcting it. It makes sense in that situation because the link was strong from the start. But in a stepfamily, where trust and familiarity take time to build, control can feel like it doesn't care or is intrusive. For a stepparent, real love frequently means holding back— choosing not to punish, not to push, and not to force a bond. It means letting your step kids deal with their feelings on their own, rather than stepping in to help them. It's a choice to be quiet when you don't have to lead a conversation. It's choosing to be present instead of being in charge. This kind of love can seem like it's not there. There are no big moments, no "look what I've done for you" moments, or anything like that. But it has a lot of power. A youngster starts to feel comfortable when they see that you aren't trying to dominate them, take their parents' place, or demand their loyalty. And safety is what enables authentic connections to form over time.

Not all acts of love look like action.

One of the most essential things stepparents can do is understand that doing less doesn't mean you care less. Going too far, especially when you weren't invited, can hurt the connections you're trying to make. In your role, love may not mean keeping things in order or correcting bad behavior. It might look like:

- Giving the child the space they need.
- Being there but not too much.

- Listening without making a judgment.
- Letting the biological parent deal with problems, even if you think you know what to do.

These quieter forms of love tend to work better in the long run. They tell the child that you're not attempting to take over, but that you're there for them whenever they're ready.

Additionally, they demonstrate to your partner that you respect the family's boundaries and want to foster peace rather than control.

Support without Wanting to Own

Being a stepparent means offering unconditional love, without needing to possess or control. It's a balancing act to give without expecting love right away, accepting that others might not be happy to see you. And still deciding to be kind and respectful.

- Possessive love states, "I've done a lot; you should be grateful to me."
- Peaceful love states, "I'm here because I care, no matter how you treat me."

You start to love more freely when you stop tying your worth to your work. You cease looking for approval from the kids or from how things are going in the house. You work from a place of emotional stability and self-worth instead. This isn't being emotionally detached.

Love as Stability, Not Control

Stepchildren don't need extra people instructing them what to do. They require parents who are always there for them, are polite, and are stable emotionally. In this case, love means being dependable—showing up every day with the same calm tone, clear limits, and consistent attitude. You don't have to be perfect. You don't have to be too loving or always involved. You need to feel protected emotionally. One of the most loving things you can do for a child, especially one who is going through changes, divorce, or instability, is to always be there for them. Your steadiness becomes a subtle way to connect. Your limits help people trust you. In a world full of stress, your neutrality is a welcome change.

Love in a blended family won't always look the same as it does in a biological family, and that's okay. That's a novel way to say things. A better one. One that makes room for actual connection, peace, and patience. Redefining love helps you stop feeling stressed, comparing yourself to others, and overexerting yourself. It allows you to honor your responsibilities and keep your energy safe while being there for others in meaningful ways. You don't have to prove anything. You don't have to chase love. You only need to follow your heart and let love bloom on its own, slowly and steadily.

The Power of Emotional Distance

When you become a stepfamily, your feelings may prompt you to give more, work harder, and endure pain for the sake of love and connection. You may feel like you have to be fully involved—caring profoundly, always being there, and demonstrating your devotion through emotional labour. Blended families take time, patience, and understanding to grow together, and putting all of your emotions into them without any limits can rapidly become too much. Over time, trying to "be there" in every aspect starts to wear down your peace of mind, especially when people don't want you to be involved or don't care. This is when emotional distance becomes not just useful, but necessary. It's not about pulling back or being distant. It's about taking care of your inner world on purpose so you can think clearly and stay healthy.

Why It's Good to Take a Break from Your Feelings

Stepparents often have to deal with feelings that aren't theirs. You might feel the same way as your stepchildren, partner, or even your partner's ex. You might not even realize it, yet you may still absorb the stress in the house. You might think of it as a personal failing when anything feels wrong. This kind of emotional involvement can lead to anxiety, disorientation, and exhaustion. Emotional distance allows you to be aware of what's going on around you without letting it affect you. You are still conscious, yet you are not devoured. You care, but not too much. You care about others without letting every difficulty that comes up in the house deplete you. This distance helps you control your reaction, maintain your perspective, and respond with thoughtfulness instead of anger.

What Is the Difference Between Distance and Disconnection?

Emotional distance and separation are not the same thing, even though they may seem similar. Disconnection is not, not caring, not wanting to get involved, or feeling apathetic. On the other hand, emotional distance is a deliberate and courteous limit. It's like an internal pause that allows you time to think before taking in anything that isn't yours. Emotional distance is the space between a stimulus and a response. A kid might get angry. There may be a problem with co-parenting. There may be a lot of tension in the room. You don't rush to solve or understand it when you are emotionally distant. You take a breath. You look. You let your partner take the lead. You don't take it personally. This area provides you with space to stay grounded. It helps you stay calm when things are emotionally out of control. Additionally, it enables you to maintain a good balance without harming your mental health.

Making Room Without Guilt

Stepparents often feel that they must demonstrate their love by always being there for their stepchildren. However, that degree of exposure isn't sustainable, especially in a family that may still be grieving, undergoing a transition, or recovering. You can keep your heart safe. When feelings are running high, you might pull back. You can step back from situations that are making you feel bad or are aimed at you. You are not a therapist, a referee, or an emotional sponge. You are a partner, which means you are a person with your emotional limits. Taking time for yourself doesn't mean you don't care; it means you're prioritizing your well-being. It means you care smartly. You care in a way that doesn't cross your lines. You care in a way that gives the biological parents time to deal with the emotional impact that they are best able to bear. And you care enough to stop yourself from getting to that point.

Clearer Emotions Make Relationships Stronger

When you start to practice emotional distance, your family relationships often improve. This is not because you are more interested, but because you are more consistent. When you have emotional clarity, you don't react to every change in the environment. You don't think less of yourself based on how the kids feel about you on any particular day. You're not saying too much, apologising too much, or going too far. You are just being yourself, and that consistency makes you someone others can trust. Kids who used to fight with you start to notice how calm you are. Instead of reacting to what you say, your partner may come to rely on you for stable support. And most crucially, you start to trust yourself again since you are no longer getting lost in an emotional world that wasn't yours to begin with. In a culture where love is often viewed as being completely emotionally involved, choosing emotional distance can initially feel unusual. But over time, you'll realize that this is one of the most loving things you can do for yourself, your partner, and even your stepchildren. Emotional distance does not mean being detached. It's being strict. It's the choice to quit being lost in how other people feel, act, and react, and get back to your emotional centre. It's the line that lets you be kind without getting too involved.

CHAPTER 3:
When You Try Too Hard You Lose Yourself

Why over-functioning backfires every time.

Mary Dixon

The Invisible Labor No One Sees

People often fail to notice or appreciate the emotional and practical effort that stepparents put in. You do the dishes, keep track of appointments, help with homework, buy groceries, and try to keep the peace. But even if you try, the thanks you think you deserve never seems to come. And slowly, without you knowing it, something inside you starts to break down. This is the weight of "invisible labor," which is the mental, emotional, and physical work you do in your job that others don't see until it ceases. It makes me tired. It makes you feel alone.

And in many cases, it can't last. The first step to resolving this situation is to understand it. Your willingness to help may originate from love and loyalty, but it can also become a trap that leaves you tired and unfulfilled.

The problem isn't the work; it's the imbalance.

The problem isn't caring for other people. The issue is doing more than your fair share without being recognized, appreciated, or even asked. You could have to clean up after other people, do things that the biological parents should do, or take on jobs that no one else sees. You do everything because you want to help, whether it's to alleviate tension or demonstrate your commitment. However, as time passes and your work goes unrecognized, the emotional toll begins to rise. You can feel ignored, unappreciated, or even like you don't exist. You start to think that if you had only done a little more, things might have gotten better. This way of thinking keeps you stuck in a loop of "over-functioning," where you do more than is good for you and get less than you need in return.

Mental Load: The Hidden Weight of Stepping In Too Often

The work you do isn't always physical. A lot of it is in your head. You could be the one who remembers birthdays, buys things you need for the house, or sets up schedules. You might think you have to run the house, keep the kids in line, or make sure your partner is happy every day. This "mental load" is tiring since it never seems to stop. Your brain is always working, even while you're not doing anything. It's planning, anticipating, and getting ready. And because this kind of work isn't visible, it doesn't get any credit. No one can see how much room it takes up in your head. No one sees how much work it takes to plan for everyone else. Resentment builds when your wants aren't addressed and your hard work goes unrecognized. You can start to pull away emotionally or wonder how much you mean to the family. That change within you a clear warning that you've lost your balance, and it's time to consider how much you're carrying and why.

Helping Others Shouldn't Mean Losing Yourself

One of the risks of doing too much is that it can cause you to fade away over time. You get so busy running the house or calming down fights that you forget who you were before you joined this family. Your interests fade away, you stop sleeping, and your sense of self becomes tied to servitude. But you should never lose who you are just to be helpful. When you think your worth is just in what you do for others, you start to believe that your worth is only in what you provide. That belief is not only wrong, but also misguided. You are more than just a role player. You are a complete person with your feelings, needs, and wants. And when you don't pay attention to those things all the time, even if you do, it might lead to burnout. You should feel like you want to make a real contribution, not like you have to. You should feel free to say yes, but you should also feel free to say no.

Taking Back Your Time and Energy

If you've been carrying too much for too long, you shouldn't continue to do more. It's time to pause, reflect on your obligations, and make conscious decisions about what you will and won't do in the future. Ask yourself this first:

- Did someone ask me to do this, or did I think it was my job?
- Is this job the biological parents?
- Am I giving up something I need to do something that no one else expects?
- Would I still do this if I didn't expect anything in return?

These questions help you get back to your center. They remind you that not every act of service is good for you and that not every donation brings people together. Sometimes, the best thing you can do for yourself and your family is to stop doing everything and start taking care of your energy. It may be customary for stepparents to do invisible work, but it should never be the norm. You're not just a background figure in your own life. You are not the quiet engine that keeps the home going. You are a person who deserves to be seen, heard, and appreciated.

Overgiving Leads to Overresenting

Many stepparents begin with an open heart and a genuine desire to help. You might prepare meals, take your stepchildren to school, manage household chores, or spend time trying to bond with them. At first, these attempts appear to have merit. You're doing your part. You're making things. You're making an effort. But after time, you can realize that the appreciation isn't there. The relationship you wanted to develop is still a long way off. Your partner's support isn't always there. The load continues becoming heavier, yet no one seems to care. What used to feel like kindness slowly turns into a burden. This is where over giving transforms into over resenting—a change that happens gradually and then suddenly in ways you didn't expect. The problem with this dynamic is that it can go unnoticed until you're emotionally spent, distant, or quietly angry. And that anger can slowly destroy both your relationship and your peace of mind if you don't deal with it.

How Much Does It Cost to Say Yes Too Often

Stepparents typically want to say yes. You want to help. You want to ensure everything goes smoothly. You need to build trust, especially if you're new to the family. But the more you say yes, especially if you don't seek or get help, the more likely you are to feel like you're being taken for granted. You may agree to things you can't do, such as watching the kids when you're already stressed, attending activities you weren't asked to, or stepping in when your partner should be in charge. Each uneven "yes" over time is like a stealthy outflow from your emotional bank account. When there is no balance, those "yes" times go from being gifts to becoming things you have to do. What started as good deeds now feels like an obligation. And when you think you have to give more than you get, you get more and more angry. That feeling of frustration isn't selfish; it's a sign that you're not respecting your limits.

Giving Out of Fear or Guilt

Many stepparents go too far because they are scared of what will happen if they don't. You might be concerned that people will perceive you as cold, distant, or uncommitted. Or maybe you want to avoid fighting with your partner, and you believe that by doing more, you might make things less tense. Guilt can often make you give too much. You could feel bad that you aren't the biological parent. Feeling bad that the kids didn't pick you. I feel bad because the family is still getting used to things. In response, you want to prove your worth by doing things for others. But when you give out of fear or guilt instead of a healthy emotional place, it never feels good. It doesn't help people connect. It doesn't make respect stronger. It just drains you and makes you feel like your worth is based on how much you do.

Resentment Is a Sign, Not a Flaw

Being resentful doesn't make you a lousy stepparent. It suggests that something crucial is being overlooked, probably your own needs. When you feel dissatisfied, it usually means you've gone too far to make other people happy. Perhaps you've been getting involved without being asked. Or you've been taking on emotional tension that isn't yours to deal with. You might be giving more time, energy, or patience than you have. The anger grows slowly, often manifesting as impatience, emotional withdrawal, or a short temper. Recognizing anger for what it is—an alert that something needs to change—is the first step in dealing with it. You can change your mind about your obligations. You can say no without giving a reason. You can set limits that safeguard your mental health, even if they change what people in the house expect of you.

Emotional Clarity Leads to Healthy Contributions

Instead of over giving, you should intentionally contribute instead of disengaging. Giving with awareness, limits, and choice keeps your energy up. You no longer donate out of fear or duty. You give because you want to and because you feel ready to. This could mean doing less around the house, letting your partner take charge more often, or spending less time with the kids. It could be making time for yourself, taking care of your personal needs, or just getting more sleep. When you make time for yourself, you become more stable, less reactive, and more emotionally present in ways that are good for you and last. You no longer hate the way your family works, since you're not giving up your own needs to deal with it. Giving too much is not love. It's typically pressure, whether it's internal or external, that makes you think your worth is based on how much you do. But being real, not trying too hard, is what makes a real, enduring connection. When you stop providing more than you can, you start to feel less angry. You will feel more energetic when you begin to respect your limits. And when you choose balance over burnout, you start coming from a place of calm, which is something every family needs, even if they don't know how to ask for it.

Doing More Doesn't Mean Being More

It's tempting to think that work equals importance in a stepfamily. You come. You help. You say yes even when you're worn out. You do your best to show that you belong by cleaning, planning, driving, and helping with assignments. It seems like the more you do, the more people will notice you. The more you give, the more others will like you. But after a while, you start to see something that worries you: the way others treat you doesn't seem to change when you give them things. The link you wanted isn't happening. You don't get the appreciation you thought you would. You still feel like an outsider in the house you help run, even if you put in all that additional work. This realization hurts, but it also sets you free. Because it shows a basic fact that every stepparent must eventually accept: your worth is not based on how much you do.

Stepparents Often Try to Earn Their Place

Stepparents often don't automatically receive the same respect and attention as biological parents. You could have thought you had to "earn" your place by doing things for others or always being there for them.

You could think that going above and beyond will show your stepchildren, your partner, or even yourself how valuable you are. This kind of thinking makes you do more than you should. You say yes when you want to say no. You take on tasks that no one asked you to do. You help out before it's needed, expecting that your dedication would bring you closer together. But you don't gain love and respect by being tired. They grow via trust, patience, and consistency, not by doing things all the time. No amount of extra work can make someone accept something or change dynamics that need time and emotional maturity.

Too Much Work Can Make You Emotionally Unstable

Doing too much, especially when you're not asked or thanked, throws off the balance in the family. You can feel that you're always giving, while others aren't doing anything. You could start to expect praise or thanks, and when you don't get it, it hurts. This imbalance makes people angry and sometimes even resentful. Not because you didn't want to assist, but because helping was your way of attempting to get attention. You feel emotionally drained and unappreciated when that demand isn't supplied. Instead of making connections, doing too much might make things tense without saying anything. You can feel angry, withdrawn, or unsure about your place in the home. These aren't signals that you've failed; they're signs that you've been assessing your worth in a way that won't last.

Being there, builds connections.

People don't connect with you because of how much you do. They connect with you when you are emotionally available, polite, and there for them—when you show up all the time, even if it's not flawless. Stepchildren, especially those who are dealing with loyalty issues or emotional changes, don't always want someone to "do" more for them. They require room, safety, and a calm person around. You can give that without going too far or bending over backwards. Your partner also doesn't require a household manager or someone who does too much for them. They need someone who knows what they can and can't do, talks plainly, and gives from a place of confidence instead of feeling like they have to. It may seem like doing more is productive, but it's not necessarily the case. In reality, letting other people take charge of their jobs and stepping aside may frequently make things healthier and build trust.

Changing Your Worth in the Family

Part of being a Nacho Parent is changing how you see your place and worth in the family. You don't have to prove anything here. You are not a parent who takes over. You don't have to worry about how comfortable, productive, or well-behaved everyone else is. You are a partner. A steady adult. Someone who has their own needs, limits, and sense of self. Your worth comes from how you act, not how much you do for other people. You can find calm when you stop linking your worth to how busy you are. You begin to give in ways that feel real and long-lasting. You stop trying to get people to like you and start enjoying being yourself. You won't be loved more if you do more. It won't speed up bonding, fix family problems, or make sure you get respect. However, being stable, grounded, and emotionally available without sacrificing oneself is the best way to maintain health in this situation. You don't need to feel like you have to prove yourself. You don't have to work hard to get people to like you. You need to set limits, respect your abilities, and let your presence, not your performance, dictate your status within the family.

The Resentment That Creeps In

Initially, anger is not usually loud. It doesn't come up in a fight or an outburst. It sneaks in gently, sneaking between unrecognized attempts and disappointed hopes. You could first think it's just tiredness or annoyance. However, as time passes, that initial feeling of discomfort gradually intensifies into something more. You start to feel like no one cares about you, or that you're not even there. What used to seem like kindness now feels like giving up. And that's when anger starts to grow. Stepparents often feel resentful when their emotions are out of whack. You might be offering more than you can handle. You may find yourself in situations that take a lot out of you without giving anything back. You can quietly take on roles that were never made evident. And even if no one is trying to take advantage of you, the effect is still the same: you feel alone in your effort.

It's Not Always About One Big Moment

Most stepparents don't wake up one day feeling angry. It grows slowly, through hundreds of small agreements. You say yes when you're exhausted. You lend a hand even when no one asks. You come even when you're not invited. You ignore it at first. But those small decisions add up. You can start to notice that your partner wants your support, but doesn't say so. Or that the kids don't appreciate you being there. You could feel like you have to say yes to everything because saying no seems selfish. These habits gradually build to emotional exhaustion and, eventually, quiet anger. It's challenging to discuss this type of anger because it doesn't stem from a single source. Instead, it's because your demands, boundaries, or contributions are repeatedly ignored or not addressed. And once that anger starts to build, it changes how you act with other people, even when you try to hide it.

The Emotional Cost of Ignoring Your Needs

Stepparents are frequently the ones who keep things going smoothly in the house and act as an emotional buffer. But if you keep putting your misery aside for the sake of tranquilly, your mental health will start to suffer. You might be less patient, more reclusive, or silently annoyed during typical conversations. You may feel emotionally detached from your partner or discover that you no longer strive to connect with your kids. It's not a weakness in your character; it's a result of emotional exhaustion. And it usually starts with needs that were never voiced out loud.

When your work isn't recognized and your voice isn't heard, you automatically feel angry. You can even start to doubt your job and ask yourself, "Why am I doing all of this if it doesn't seem to matter?"

Resentment Hurts Relationships—Quietly and Slowly

Resentment differs from a dispute because it is internal and not always evident. It's not something that can be easily discussed, which makes it challenging to address; however, it's pretty harmful if left unaddressed. Resentment puts up walls between you and the ones you love. It makes you and your partner feel emotionally distant from each other. It can keep you from really connecting with your stepchildren. It even makes you lose touch with who you are—your happiness, your purpose, and your sense of belonging. Often, partners and children are unaware that animosity is building. From their point of view, everything might be OK. That's why it's essential to clearly and gently express what you need. When you start to name your limits and step back from projects or positions that are depleting you, you change the way things work, not only for yourself but also for everyone else.

Resentment Is a Sign That Things Need to Change

It's essential to recognize that being angry is not something to be ashamed of. It isn't a flaw. It's not a sign that you're failing. It means that something has to change. If you start to feel frustrated more often than satisfied, it's time to stop and think about it:

- Are you saying 'yes' when you want to say 'no'?
- Do you expect thanks that never come?
- Are you doing things that aren't your job?
- Are you avoiding talks that could help you understand things better?

The first step to getting over anger is to answer these questions honestly. Once you see that things are out of balance, you may start to set stronger limits, tell people what you can handle, and stop doing things that make you tired. This doesn't mean leaving your family; it means "walking back to yourself." As a stepparent, you don't have to let resentment take over your life. You can return to a state of balance and calm by recognizing it early, identifying its source, and making intentional changes. You can want more than just staying alive. You have the right to find happiness, connection, and emotional safety in your home. And you don't have to work hard all the time to get them.

Mary Dixon

CHAPTER 4
Let the Bio Parents Handle It

They made the children. Let them raise them.

Speak to Your Partner, Not the Kids

It's completely natural to want to step in when something feels off, especially in the early stages of blending families. When a child is being rude, breaking rules, or picking fights, the instinct to correct, guide, or discipline can feel immediate — after all, you're trying to create structure and find your place in the home. But in stepfamilies, even well-meaning interventions can sometimes backfire. When you address issues not directly related to your relationship with your stepchildren, it can unintentionally trigger defensiveness, frustration, or emotional distance. It's not that your concerns aren't valid — it's that, in their eyes, you may not be the person they expect or want correction from. Instead of talking to the kids directly, discuss the issue with your partner privately. This small but essential change respects the family's current structure and keeps you out of emotional crossfire that isn't yours.

Resistance Comes from Correction Without Connection

Bio parents with a long-term emotional relationship to the child disciplines them, it is most effective. That bond isn't typically present in most stepfamilies, especially during the first few months or years. That implies that any reprimand can feel rude, even if you are being polite and sensible. The way a stepparent corrects a youngster can make the message hard to understand. The youngster doesn't just hear the words; they also feel the power difference. They could ask why someone who isn't their primary parent is taking on a role of authority. People may think you're overstepping even if you have good intentions. That's why it's essential to let your partner, who is the child's biological parent, take the lead in behavior issues. Children are more likely to trust, feel comfortable with, and feel safe around them. Your role isn't to punish; it's to observe, consider, and discuss problems with your spouse in private so they can act from a position of appropriate authority.

Private Conversations Keep the Peace

When anything in the house makes you mad, such as a comment, a behavior, or someone ignoring a rule, it can be tempting to deal with it right away. But doing it in front of other people, especially kids, can backfire. It makes everyone nervous, encourages fighting, and creates tension between you and the kids for no apparent reason. Instead, remember what happened and discuss it later with your spouse in a calm manner. This approach isn't passive; it's deliberate. You are picking the moment, place, and tone that will make your concern likely to be noticed and fixed. You can say this in that private space:

- "I didn't like how she talked to me today. "Can you talk to her about it?"
- "He didn't do what he was supposed to do again.

Can we discuss how to handle that together?
- "I need your help setting limits on this issue." I don't want to be the one who makes it happen.

This form of communication keeps the focus where it should be: on the people who are in charge of running the house, not on the stepparent and the child.

How to Keep Relationships Safe and Avoid Power Struggles

When a stepparent talks directly to a child, especially about discipline, it may lead to power issues. Kids could push the limits, fight back, or shut off emotionally. Those moments don't help people trust each other; they hurt it. However, when the biological parent intervenes, the youngster may not appreciate the correction, but they know who is in charge. The expectation is more obvious. The emotional setting is familiar. And most significantly, it keeps you from doing something you were never meant to do. You maintain a strong emotional bond with the child by refraining from direct correction. You stay calm and impartial, so children don't think of you as someone who punishes or puts pressure on them. Over time, this calm, low-conflict attitude helps build trust and connection, which is something that coercive authority never does.

Taking a Step Back Shows Strength

To stay out of the parenting dynamic, you need to be sure of yourself and clear. At first, you could think you're not accomplishing enough or that you're avoiding your responsibilities. But really, you're picking a job that helps the family without getting in the way of others who didn't ask for your leadership. Taking a step back doesn't imply being quiet; it means being mindful of when and where to speak up. You're talking to the appropriate person (your partner) at the right time (in private) and in the correct way (together). This is what reasonable limits look like. This is how to protect your energy. This is how to show up strong, clear-headed, and emotionally mature. By talking to your partner instead of disciplining the kids directly, you maintain your role, your tranquilly, and your long-term relationships with everyone involved. You let the biological parent take the lead, which puts you in a better and more sustainable position. You don't have to yell to be heard. You don't have to make them follow the rules to get respect. Just stay grounded, communicate effectively, and believe that your partner will step up when the opportunity arises.

Scripts for Stepping Back Gracefully

When things are tense, expectations aren't clear, or emotions are running high, one of the hardest things for stepparents to do is know what to say. You can feel like you have to respond, explain yourself, or correct someone's behavior because it's what you always do or because you're angry. However, with Nacho Parenting, the goal isn't to gain control; it's to maintain a clear, calm, and emotionally stable environment. It's essential to learn how to step back verbally and intentionally. Having a few prepared statements or "scripts" ready will help you avoid unnecessary conflict while still being polite and present. These scripts aren't about getting out of doing your duty; they're about putting it where it belongs: with the biological parents. You can use these scripts and examples in real life.

When a Child Doesn't Listen to You or Breaks a Rule

When a child talks back, defies a rule, or crosses a queue, it makes you feel bad. You might want to step in and correct them, but if there's not much trust yet, it could easily backfire. Let your partner take the lead instead. Say this:

- "Your mum or dad will need to talk to you about that."
- "I'm going to let your parent take care of this."
- "We can ask your mum or dad about that."
- "I'm not the right person to give my opinion here."

These answers are clear and calm. They don't make things worse. They don't put the child to the test. They make it plain that someone else is responsible for making things right, without making a fuss.

When Someone Asks You to Make a Decision, You Shouldn't Own

Kids might ask you things like, "Can I go to my friend's house?" or "Can I stay up later tonight?" These requests, while benign, might put stepparents in a tricky place. You want to help, but saying yes can cause misunderstanding or even make things tense with the biological parent if your answer is different from theirs. Instead of making the call, politely turn down the offer. Answer with:

- "That's something you should ask your dad/mom."
- "Let's ask your parent about that."
- "I don't know what your mum or dad wants, so

I'll let them choose."
- "Why don't you ask your parent and tell me what they say?"

This keeps you neutral and makes sure that the right people are talking to each other. You're not getting rid of the child; you're just changing who is responsible for it.

When You're Overwhelmed or Forced into a Role You Didn't Want to Be in

Sometimes, a partner or family member may think you're free to help out with parenting duties like driving, keeping track of chores, or dealing with a behavior problem. If this happens frequently, you need to speak clearly, not angrily. Say these calm boundary-setting things:

- "I'm happy to help when I can, but we need to talk about what we expect from each other going forward."
- "I want to help you, but I can't take on tasks that make me tired or stressed."
- "Let's talk about what seems fair and long-lasting for both of us."

- "This might be something you and the kids should talk about."

You should only use these scripts when speaking privately with your partner, not in front of the children. They assist in setting new limits without blaming anyone or escalating the situation.

When You Need Some Time or Space to Get Your Act Together

You may need to walk away at times, not to dodge something, but to show yourself respect. It's fine to leave a situation gracefully if it becomes too hot, uncomfortable, or emotionally challenging. Say something like this:

- "I'm going to give this space a minute."
- "I have to leave and let you take care of this."
- "I care, but I can't respond right now."
- "I'll get back to you later." For now, I'm going to back off.

These statements aren't frigid; they're well-thought-out. They show you how to manage your emotions and prevent you from acting in ways that could harm your relationships. They also show that you prefer peace over chaos. What you say and what you choose not to say can change the whole emotional atmosphere of your home when you live in a blended family. Taking a step back doesn't mean going away; it means taking a closer look. It involves being careful with your words, moving responsibility with respect, and keeping true to your limits. Scripts are not walls; they are tools. They help you get through tough times with confidence and lower the chance of a fight. They remind you of your position without saying sorry and encourage others to take responsibility for what is theirs to manage.

Not Your Job = Not Your Responsibility

One of the most freeing facts about living in a stepfamily is also one of the toughest to accept: just because something needs to be done doesn't mean you have to do it. In mixed families, it's easy for obligations to get mixed up. Stepparents often feel like they have to take on tasks that aren't their job, such as discipline, logistics, emotional support, or ordinary parenting activities, when there are no clear boundaries. However, taking on roles that were never yours to begin with doesn't make you feel connected; it
creates an imbalance. The Nacho Parenting method says that if something isn't your job, you don't have to do it. And that doesn't mean you don't care. It makes you aware.

Knowing the Difference Between Ownership and Support

There is a big difference between giving help and taking charge. Support means you're ready to help when asked or when it seems reasonable for you. When you own something, you feel like you have to take care of things that no one asked you to, even if they belong to the biological parent. It's vital to remember that helping someone once doesn't imply you have to do it for the rest of your life. You don't have to drive the kids to and from school every day just because you picked them up one day. Just because you cook dinner a couple of nights a week doesn't imply you're the family chef. If you jump in when things are tense, you don't have to be the one to mediate the situation. People often think you're okay with doing these things without talking to them formally. Then, when you start to feel overwhelmed or unappreciated, resentment starts to build—not because you don't care, but because you're doing work that was never really yours.

How to Avoid the Trap of Silent Responsibility

Silent responsibility means doing things without being asked or recognized, taking care of things just because no one else has. This may seem necessary at first, but it becomes a problem when it becomes a habit. This could look like this in stepfamilies:

- Doing schoolwork because no one else will do it.
- Taking care of meal planning, routines, or holiday plans.
- Setting up communication between families or

settling disagreements about parenting.

You might have thought, "Someone has to do it," or "I'm just trying to help." However, when these things happen without being discussed and are unfair, they become expected. Over time, it's not just that you're performing the work; it's that you're now seen as responsible for it, even if you never committed to doing it in the first place. When you set limits, it doesn't mean you stop assisting. It implies that you cease taking on duties that are emotionally or practically taxing and not part of your job responsibilities.

Allowing the Right Person to Take Charge

It's easy to want to step in when a biological parent doesn't do their job or ignores it. You want things to go well. You want the home to feel safe and secure. But every time you step up and someone else steps back, you're making it easier for them to stay passive and more complicated for you to handle. Allowing the correct person to deal with the problem requires trusting the family system, even when it's challenging. It could mean letting your partner forget something and then having to deal with the consequences. It could be watching a situation unfold badly without rushing to correct it. It takes strength to hold back like this. But it also puts the emotional weight back where it belongs. People are more inclined to grow, adapt, and interact on purpose when they are given complete responsibility for their roles. You won't see that increase if you keep making up for every setback.

You Have Permission to Put Yourself First

When stepparents opt not to help, they often feel guilty because they don't want to be perceived as selfish or uninterested. But there's a distinction between neglecting your family and keeping your emotional bandwidth. You aren't here to take care of someone. You are here to develop a life with your partner and engage in activities that are healthy and manageable. You can ask yourself:

- Is this my job?
- Am I emotionally ready for this right now?
- Will my participation make things clearer or more confusing?
- Am I jumping in because I want to, or because I feel like I have to?

You'll start to see what's yours to carry and what's not when you answer honestly. And from there, you may begin to set limits that make you feel strong instead of weak. Taking on too much doesn't make you a better stepparent. Taking on other people's responsibilities doesn't make you more loving. You are not more important because you do the labor that other people don't want to do. You can say, "This isn't my job." You can take a step back. You can choose serenity over performance if you want. You're not only guarding your time; you're also protecting your relationships, your mental well-being, and your overall vitality.

Trusting Your Partner to Step Up

Letting go of control and letting your partner, who is the biological parent, take full responsibility for their parenting role is one of the most challenging but most crucial things to do as a Nacho Parent. This can be scary for many stepparents.

- What if they don't do it the way you want them to?
- What if they don't pay attention to anything that needs to be dealt with?
- What if their method is inconsistent, too laid-back, or excessively emotional?

These worries are real. You want the house to run smoothly. You wish to help and lead the kids. However, jumping in every time your partner falls short doesn't solve the problem; it merely hides it. When you stop making up for someone else's lack of action and start expecting them to be responsible, that's when proper balance in a blended family begins.

Letting Go of Control Doesn't Mean Letting Go of Care

It's hard to let go of things you've done because you had to, because you were used to it, or because you loved it. You might have been the one in charge of the discipline, routines, or emotional check-ins because it was simpler for you, or maybe your spouse wasn't doing what they were supposed to do. However, as time passes, this arrangement begins to wear you down emotionally. You don't have to leave the relationship or appear as though you don't care if you trust your partner to step up. It means putting the blame back where it belongs. You're not quitting; you're deciding to stop being responsible for someone else's job. Your partner can completely take on their obligations without you continually buffering the consequences if you choose this option.

Why They Need to Be in Charge

When stepparents take up parenting chores, the biological parent may not even realize it, but they may stop being involved. The more you do, the more they pull away. This imbalance causes stress and prevents you from fulfilling your duties properly. Kids also benefit when their biological parent is the one who sets limits, guides behavior, and gives emotional support. It strengthens the bond between parents and children, making it easier to understand who is in charge at home. You're not putting distance between you and your partner by letting them lead. You're making things more straightforward. You're building a system where kids know who is in charge of them, allowing you to focus on maintaining a peaceful and polite relationship with everyone in the house.

How to Show That You Trust Them in Real Life

Trust doesn't mean following orders without question or being quiet. It's a conscious choice followed by consistent action. In this case, it means:

- Allowing them to discipline their child, even if it takes longer than you'd want.
- Don't discuss regulations or consequences with the kids on the side.
- Keeping your worries to yourself until you can discuss them with your partner calmly and confidentially.
- Not correcting your partner's parenting approach on the spot, even if you would do it differently.

If they don't do anything, you can politely show your anger by saying:

- "I need to know that you can take care of this." We need to be on the same page since I'm stepping aside from being a parent.
- "This is affecting the family." "Can you talk to them about it soon?"
- "I'll let you know if I see behavior that crosses the line, but I won't be the one to punish you."

It's not about blaming your partner in these talks. They're about creating a new dynamic that keeps you calm and gives you more power to be a parent.

Be Patient While They Get Back to Work

It can be challenging to relinquish your role, especially if you've been the default for a long time. Your partner may need some time to adjust to it. They can trip, put things off, or even refuse to step in at first. That's normal. What matters is that you stick to your decision to step back. Discomfort is often a part of growth. If your partner starts to feel the pressure of having to lead without you, it can be just what they need to take their job more seriously. When you quit stepping in, they start to understand that someone else won't always take care of the problem. That's when actual change happens, not because you made it happen, but because you trusted the process and let them grow. Trusting your partner to stand up doesn't mean giving up your principles; it means trusting them to step into theirs. It's a sign of faith in their ability to lead and in your right to stand back without feeling bad about it. As you continue on your Nacho Parenting adventure, keep in mind that your strength doesn't come from how much you do, but from how effectively you safeguard your role, your energy, and your mental health. And as you make room, you'll start to notice something powerful: your partner will either rise or have the chance to.

Mary Dixon

CHAPTER 5:

You're Not the Household Manager

Stepping back from logistics, chores, and emotional overload.

Stop Doing All the Driving, Cooking, and Planning

Often, stepparents end up being the primary caregivers in stepfamilies. You start by helping out, such as picking up the kids from school, cooking a couple of meals a week, or keeping the calendar organized so everything runs smoothly. Initially, you may feel like you're making a difference. But after a while, what you do becomes an expectation. The more you do, the less you notice how hard you're working and how much responsibility you have. You soon realize that you are the one who keeps things running smoothly: driving the kids around, making meals, making appointments, and managing the everyday flow of family life. Not because you were asked, but because no one else did. This insidious buildup of too much to accomplish doesn't simply make you tired; it may also erode your sense of self. Nacho Parenting provides you the freedom to stop worrying about things that aren't yours to deal with. You are not the child's parent. You are not the family secretary, the chef, or the driver. You are a partner, not a free household manager.

When Help Turns Into a Hidden Burden

Stepparents typically say yes because they want to be kind and supportive. You don't want to change routines. You want to help. You might even like being helpful. But there is a thin line between being useful and being misused. It's time to stop and ask yourself if you're doing most of the travelling to and from school, cooking most of the meals, or planning every family function.

- Was this my job in the first place?
- Am I in charge because no one else will be?
- Am I giving up my own tranquilly to keep it all together?

When these duties become second nature, they become out of balance. And silent duties often develop into unspoken anger.

The Family Doesn't Need a Hero

You might think that the house would fall apart if you stopped taking care of it, but that attitude can exacerbate bad habits. The truth is that if you've been in charge, other people have just worked around your work. That doesn't mean you're the only one who can accomplish it. You are the one who has been the most willing. Their biological parents should be in charge of their children. When it comes to their children, your partner should be in charge of most family arrangements. You probably did those things because there was a gap and you filled it. But carrying that load for a long time, especially if it's hurting your mental or physical health, isn't honorable; it's not going to last. Letting go of that control doesn't mean giving up; it means giving other people the chance to grow into their roles.

What It Means to Step Back

Taking a break from regular tasks doesn't mean you don't care; it means you're taking care of yourself. It means you start to make choices about how you spend your time and energy. You stop thinking that you'll always be the one to cook, drive, or plan, and start establishing limits on what you can and can't do. It might sound like:

- "I can't drive today." "Can you set up something else?"
- "Let's take turns cooking dinner or come up with a plan for meals that change every week."
- "I'm not in charge of the school project's

schedule." That should be between you and your kid.

These are not threats. They are polite changes that change your place in the family. They give ownership back to the people who should have it and let you stop performing work that no one else recognizes.

Giving Yourself Space Again

When you do too much in your home, you don't have much time for your objectives, rest, or creativity. If you're always on the go—driving from one location to another and mentally balancing the week's tasks—you steadily lose touch with who you are. You don't have to make a big scene to reclaim your time. It starts with little things:

- Not feeling bad about taking a night off from cooking.
- Allowing your partner to take care of their child's transportation.
- Saying no to planned gatherings that don't meet your current requirements.

Every time you reclaim a piece of your energy, you prove that you are a person, not just a position. And when you take care of your time, your happiness begins to return. You find time to rest, breathe, and reconnect with the person you were before you got caught up in all the logistics. You don't have to be the planner, driver, or caretaker. You are a partner with limits, not a worker in the house. You don't have to make everything work; you can choose how much you want to help. Let other people perform their jobs. Teach the kids how to be independent. Allow your partner to take on all of the responsibilities of becoming a parent. You are valuable to your family not because of what you do, but because of the peace you provide when you are balanced and not burned out.

When Helping Turns into Enabling

Your desire to help as a stepparent may stem from a genuine concern. You want the house to work. You want your partner and stepkids to know that you care about them. You might step in when something needs to be done or volunteer to help when things seem too much. But what starts as kindness can rapidly turn into a cycle that makes you feel too much and leaves others feeling not enough. It's time to ask yourself, "Is my support empowering others, or is it letting them back off?" when your helpfulness becomes the glue that holds everything together. It's easy to cross the line between being helpful and becoming a crutch. If you breach a line, the aid you give may start to encourage behavior that allows others to perform less than they should, which may eventually lead to irritation and imbalance.

How Enabling Works in Stepfamilies

Enabling doesn't always look like bad behavior; it can also appear as being helpful, dependable, and committed. However, beneath the surface, there is a gradual erosion of responsibility. If you let other people depend on you too much, they won't be able to learn how to be responsible for their roles. In a blended family, enabling could look like:

- Taking care of school routines that your spouse should be in charge of.
- Cleaning up after youngsters who can do it themselves.
- Always the one to fix problems or misunderstandings.
- Dealing with the emotional impact of something you didn't do.
- Doing things yourself since it's "just easier" than waiting for someone else.

At the time, it can seem like it's working. However, over time, these behaviors can make you dependent instead of helping you grow, and you wind up carrying the weight that isn't yours.

The Emotional Cost of Helping Too Much

When you continually step in to help others, your own needs often go unmet. You might feel tired, angry, or silently resentful. You might even start to pull away emotionally, not because you want to, but because you don't have enough time. This form of quiet burnout might make you feel distant from your partner and cause problems with your stepchildren. It could also make you wonder what your place is in the family. You can think that you're giving everything and getting very little in return. It's even worse that your hard work might not even be noticed, even though you meant well. People typically cease thanking you for your continued help once they become accustomed to it. What was once valued is now expected to be. And when you stop being grateful, you rapidly get angry.

Why People Should Have to Deal with the Results of Their Actions

One of the reasons enabling is so bad is that it takes away the natural repercussions that people need to feel. If your partner forgets to check the school calendar and you always fill in the gap, they won't learn to pay more attention to their responsibilities. If a youngster won't do their duties and you do them anyway because you're angry, they won't understand how their decisions effect the household. When you jump in, you might be teaching the people around you that they don't have to show up because you'll always be there. It can be challenging to let others feel bad or fail at first. But it has to be done. It allows children to learn, grow, and be responsible for their actions. It also teaches children that you don't have to help them all the time and that you won't keep doing things that aren't your job.

Moving from Helper to Partner

You don't have to quit helping completely. However, you need to plan your support, not automate it. To start that change, ask yourself a few essential questions:

- Is this my job, or am I just filling in for someone else?
- Am I assisting because I want to or because I have to?
- What would happen if I took a step back?
- Would someone else be willing to help?
- Have I ever made it plain what I will and won't do?

Speak honestly with your partner from now on. Tell them where you feel like you're doing too much and where you'd want to see more shared responsibility. Give them a chance to move up, even if their idea of "stepping up" isn't precisely the same as yours. When you help with defined goals and limits, it can be a beautiful thing. However, when it becomes enabling, it progressively drains your energy, throws things off balance, and prevents others from growing. As a stepparent, you don't have to take care of all the emotional and practical needs of the family. It's to help in ways that make sense for you, while trusting others to do their part. You give the family a chance to grow up when you stop enabling them and start stepping back. You also get back the energy you were never meant to lose.

Letting Go of the "Default Parent" Identity

In many stepfamilies, a quiet yet strong dynamic begins to emerge. The stepparent, often unintentionally, becomes the one everyone turns to for help with everyday needs, emotional support, and problem-solving. You can end up doing things that you weren't expressly told to do over time. You get the kids up, make meals, keep track of the calendar, keep an eye on their routines, and deal with problems that the biological parents should be dealing with. This role, unofficially referred to as the "default parent," evolves. There is no title or accompanying conversation. It just happens. You fill in the gaps, you take charge when no one else does, and before you realize it, you're acting like the primary career in a family that isn't yours.

- What's the problem?

You never said you would do this job. And it's probably having a bigger effect on your mental health than you think.

How to Be the Default Parent in a Stepfamily

In a typical two-parent home, the default parent is often the one who does most of the behind-the-scenes labor, such as providing meals, reminding kids to do their homework, keeping their emotions in check, and making decisions. This role is especially more challenging in stepfamilies because the stepparent doesn't have the same amount of authority, history, or trust with the kids. You might still discover yourself:

- Being the first person youngsters look to for everyday needs.
- Taking care of the house when your partner is busy with other things.
- Automatically keeping an eye on rules, procedures, and duties.
- Taking care of everyone's emotional health.

This imbalance may have been necessary, but it can't last. It's not yours to keep, which is more essential. Being in a partnership that supports you doesn't imply you have to be the primary parent.

What Happens and Why It Needs to Stop

The default parent identity often arises when someone is absent or not performing their job effectively. Your partner may be busy, emotionally unavailable, or not accustomed to being a parent on their own. Instead of letting the building fall apart, you fill in the hole. You become the one who can be counted on, the one who keeps things stable. But what starts as caring becomes a weighty, never- ending obligation that you never really intended to take on. Taking on this role may seem beneficial, even praiseworthy. But it makes things unhealthy for you and everyone else. The kids could become dependent on you and not respect your limits. Your partner might not even know they're taking a step back. What about you? You feel drained emotionally and don't know where you fit in with the family. It's not selfish to let go of this role; it's vital. It's a return to clarity, where you act like an adult who is there to help, not a parent.

The Emotional Cost of Taking on a Role That Isn't Yours

It's frustrating when people always rely on you to keep the house running. You may feel like you're not there, as if you're working too hard, or as if you're emotionally weak. You might ignore your needs to keep the peace, or you might be angry because no one notices how hard you work. It's not simply the things you're doing that're bothering you; it's the unspoken pressure to always be available, organized, calm, and focused. Over time, this stress turns into quiet fatigue. You can pull away from your partner, lose your cool with the kids, or even start to question your place in the home. This is not a failure. If you feel this way, it means you're not living in a way that's good for you. It is a sign of self-respect to step away from the default parent persona. It doesn't mean leaving the family; it means letting the biological parent take the lead and adjusting your involvement on your terms.

How to Let Go of the Role and Get Your Balance Back

Letting go doesn't mean you can walk away from your duties right away. It involves being careful about where you step and where you don't. It starts with setting clear boundaries and not apologizing for them. You could say:

- "I've come to terms with the fact that I've taken on more than I can handle." I need to take a break from some of these things.

- "I can help out sometimes, but I can't be the one in charge of everything."
- "I don't want to be in charge of this, and I think we should find a better way to split up the work."

These talks might be uncomfortable, especially if other people are used to you being there. But they are necessary to change what you expect. When you step back, give yourself room to be uncomfortable. Your partner may require some time to adjust to it. The children might not want to change. That's OK. Have faith that stepping back makes an opportunity for others to stand up. If you stop being the default parent, it doesn't mean you're giving up; it means you're getting genuine. You're learning what's fair, healthy, and what works in the long run. You are choosing to help your family without sacrificing who you are in the process. It's not about doing less; it's about doing what's best for your mental health. You come back to yourself when you stop carrying more than you should. And from that peaceful space, you may go into the house with clarity, strength, and a real sense of presence.

Allowing Others to Carry Their Weight

In many stepfamily situations, the stepparent discreetly becomes the one who keeps things stable. You fill in the gaps, keep things organized, and deal with the emotional weight to keep everything going. But when you're the most responsible person in the room, people frequently
automatically start to do less because they can. The longer this pattern persists, the more tired and out of balance the house becomes. And even though it may seem like you're keeping things together, what you're doing is keeping other people from having to learn how to handle their problems. Letting go and letting others bear their weight doesn't mean giving up or not caring. It means making room for growth, taking on responsibility, and fostering a healthy family dynamic. You don't have to do everything. Things don't fall apart when you stop; they start to realign.

Doing too much can make you less likely to participate.

When one individual always jumps in to fix things, other people cease feeling like they need to do anything. Your partner might think it's taken care of if you constantly drive the kids to school. They may never find out the information if you handle the family calendar. If you do chores that no one else does, they might not even notice them. This isn't necessarily a bad thing; it's generally just a habit. But the result is the same: the responsibility falls on you, and the other people in the house become less active.

You have to be okay with being uncomfortable if you want to cease over-functioning. That could indicate that the laundry builds up. The schedule is missed. For a short while, the house doesn't run as smoothly. But it's in that place that other people start to realize what's been done for them without them knowing it, and begin to take responsibility.

Everyone Has a Job—If You Let Them

Assigning tasks that are suitable for a child's age is beneficial for them. Your partner should be taking on their parenting role entirely. And you feel better when you quit doing things that weren't meant for you. When you make room, other people will naturally start to fill it. But you have to fight the impulse to jump in when things don't go "your way" or on your schedule. Letting others carry their weight implies trusting that they can, even if they haven't yet demonstrated it. This doesn't mean that everything will be great. It means that the structure will ultimately show a more honest balance of duty. And from there, respect for each other starts to grow.

Changing What "Helping" Means

You don't have to do the most to help. It doesn't mean repairing what others ignore or covering up the effects of someone else's inaction. What real help looks like:

- Pushing your partner to take the lead and then stepping back when they do.
- Letting kids face the natural consequences of their actions instead of stopping them.
- Not feeling bad about saying "no" when something isn't your job.
- Letting others make mistakes without rushing in to fix them.

Helping is more effective when you do it intentionally, in small amounts, and with respect for yourself and your family. It's not about doing everything. It's not about doing what you think you should do; it's about doing what makes sense.

Giving Power Through Responsibility

Letting people do their part also helps them feel more confident. When your partner starts taking care of the house without being asked, it reminds them of their capabilities. Children learn to be independent and resilient when they take on their responsibilities, plan their days, or accept accountability for their actions. When you stand back, it's not because you don't like them; it's because you believe in what they can do. It means, "I trust you to handle this." People often excel when given responsibilities. This process could take a long time and not go well, but it's worth it. Not just for your peace of mind, but also for the health of everyone in the house in the long run. You were never designed to handle all of the emotional, physical, and mental stress of a family on your own. When you let others carry their weight, you're not just shielding yourself. You're also providing everyone a chance to learn, contribute, and connect by sharing responsibilities. Taking a step back doesn't imply you're less involved; it means your involvement is more important. It lets you show up because you want to, not because you have to. And in that change, you regain your time, energy, and sense of equilibrium.

Mary Dixon

CHAPTER 6:
Don't Discipline – That's Not Your Lane

Discipline should never come from the step-parent.

Mary Dixon

Kids Don't Want a New Authority

There's often an underlying question among blended families: "Who's in charge of these kids?" You might feel the stress of that question more than anybody else as a stepparent. You want to help. You want things to go well at home. When the kids act out, break rules, or test limits, you can even feel like you have to "step up." But here's something every stepparent needs to remember: discipline is not your responsibility, and it shouldn't be. Kids don't want discipline from someone they don't see as a parent, and they typically won't accept it. It can hurt the relationship before it ever has a chance to blossom if you try to correct, punish, or take control. The main principle behind Nacho Parenting is simple but powerful: "Not your kids, not your job." And that's especially true when it comes to discipline.

People Often Don't Want Discipline without Emotional History

Biological parents punish their children from a place of long-term connection. Years of caring for one another, making memories together, and loving each other. Kids generally accept discipline, even when it's painful to hear, since it comes from someone they trust. Stepparents don't have that foundation, at least not initially. Even if you live in the same house and are married to one of their parents, you haven't earned the right to correct them in their eyes. Building that trust takes time, and assuming a disciplinary role may lead to resistance, emotional withdrawal, or even defiance. People see you as the "outsider" trying to control something you didn't help make. Kids don't respond to that with warmth; they put up walls.

Why Stepparents Shouldn't Be in Charge of Discipline

When a youngster crosses a border or breaks a rule, it seems reasonable to correct their behavior. It doesn't hit the same way as it would from a biological parent. You don't have to let disorder take over the house. It implies you stick to your own business and trust your spouse to do the same. Your job is to share your worries with your partner in private and let them handle the discipline. You're not being lazy. You're being smart. You are protecting the relationship you want to develop. You're avoiding power struggles that only make things worse.

Kids Are Dealing with Loyalty Issues

One reason kids don't listen to their stepparents is that it makes them feel like they have to choose between two loyalties. A lot of kids, especially those who are still getting used to their parents' divorce or separation, feel that they are stuck between two homes, two parents, and two mental worlds. As a stepparent, if you try to reprimand them, they can think that accepting your authority means betraying their birth parent. It often makes children defensive and distant, rather than bringing them together. They can stop talking to you, ignore you, or even shut down altogether. This isn't because they are disrespectful, but rather because they don't understand your role. Staying out of the discipline lane helps clear up this emotional mess. It allows kids room to figure out who you are and who you aren't without feeling like they have to prove their loyalty.

What to Do Instead of Punishing

So what can you do when a child's actions hurt you directly? Nacho Parenting suggests redirecting, talking to, and setting boundaries without resorting to punishment. This is what that would sound like:

- "Hey, I saw that you left your stuff all around the kitchen. Could you please tidy that up before dinner?
- "That tone doesn't sit well with me." I'm going to leave and discuss this with your parent.
- "It seems like you're having trouble following the rules." Let's talk about it with your mum or dad.

And then you stop. You tell your partner about the problem. You let them take on the role of parent. By not becoming the boss, you protect your energy and your connection. This method makes it clear to everyone in the house what your job is and what it isn't. Kids don't need someone else telling them what to do all the time. They need grown-ups who are safe and respect their feelings and their space. You don't establish trust by forcing people to do things; you build it by being there, not by controlling, but by being consistent. You don't lose your importance when you stop being a disciplinarian; you gain trust. You let your partner take full responsibility for their children's growth, and you work on developing a connection that will last much longer than any punishment or timeout could.

Discipline = Bio Parents' Job

Someone in every family needs to take charge of setting rules and expectations, and ensuring everyone follows them. However, in blended families, the lines of power can become fuzzy, especially when stepparents feel compelled to act like real parents. When things get out of hand or people are rude, you can feel like you have to step in and take charge. But here's the truth: it's not your role as a stepparent to punish the kids; that's the job of the biological parent. That role comes with a history, emotional trust, and a base that can't be rushed. When the person who helped nurture and develop the child gives them correction, they are much more likely to accept, process, and respect it. As a stepparent, trying to maintain peace in the house often leads to tension, emotional distancing, and a breakdown of household harmony. Nacho Parenting reminds you that being an adult in the house doesn't mean you should be the one to set the rules.

Biological Parents Have the Most Power

A biological parent has built-in power that a stepparent does not. They've helped their child grow emotionally for years. They set expectations, showed how to act, and laid the groundwork for rules and penalties. Even when it's hard to hear, a child knows that their parent loves them when they chastise them. You haven't earned that role as a stepparent, and it's not your fault. You can't borrow power. The child could feel puzzled, defensive, or resistant, but not because the rule is harsh; it's because the person enforcing it doesn't feel "safe" or like they deserve it. It's not about who you are or what you want; it's about trust. When discipline is linked to a strong, personal relationship, it is most effective. The biological parent possesses that. And that's why they should be the ones to deal with it.

Discipline without Emotional Equity Doesn't Work

Think about how it would feel to be corrected by someone you don't entirely trust or feel close to. You are much more likely to resist their message, even if it is true. That's what occurs when a stepparent punishes a child without first creating a connection that supports their authority. The child may feel that they are being judged or targeted. They might think you're trying to take their parents' position or take power that you didn't deserve. If you get involved, the situation can escalate into a power battle, even if the rule is fair. These times don't teach; they split people up. You give the child time to think about the reprimand in a familiar, emotionally stable setting by letting the biological parent handle discipline. You're not giving up on structure; you're just letting the person who is greatest at it do it.

The Partner Conversation: A Private Leadership Reset

If you live in a house where you have to be the one to discipline everyone, it's time to have an honest talk with your partner. It can be challenging, especially if you've been in that role for a while. But it has to be done. Be calm, clear, and kind when you do it. Say this:

- "I want us to be clear about our roles going forward." I'm going to stop being strict so you can be the parent.
- "I'll help you in private, but I can't be the one to correct your child directly anymore."
- "I care about our relationship and my peace of mind." This adjustment will help keep both safe.

You're not blaming; you're realigning. You're trusting your partner to be responsible for their position as a parent and making it clear that you will still support them, but not by correcting or enforcing rules.

Your job is to be a calming presence, not a force for change.

You still retain power even if you stop being strict. You must be in the house. Your tone is essential. Your reliability is crucial. You can set limits in your area, talk to others with respect, and demonstrate emotional maturity without punishing them or acting as the enforcer. You can say:

- I'm going to leave and talk to your parent.
- "I'm not happy with the way things are going right now. "Let's take a break."
- "That's something your mum or dad should talk to you about."

These answers keep you calm and put the blame where it belongs. You're not avoiding problems; you're just ensuring you understand your position. In Nacho Parenting, not being strict isn't a sign of weakness; it's a sign of wisdom. When discipline comes from the person who made the rules, it is most effective. When someone else tries to enforce them, it doesn't work as well. By taking a step back, you conserve your energy, maintain a strong relationship with the child, and reinforce the parenting structure within the family. You are not the one who makes the rules. You are an adult who supports them, a partner, and a solid presence, not a parent. And when you stop attempting to control, you make room for connection, peace, and trust that will last.

Staying Calm, Not Confrontational

One of the most valuable things a stepparent can learn is how to remain calm when emotions run high. Your ability to stand your ground without making things worse is more important than any punishment or order. This is true whether your kids are fighting, a teenager rolls their eyes, or you disagree with a parenting decision. There will always be problems in a blended family. People are quite emotional, and there are a lot of misunderstandings; loyalties are also split. However, when you choose to remain calm instead of addressing every problem immediately, you create an emotionally safe environment for yourself and others. Being peaceful doesn't mean being quiet or letting bad behavior go. It involves deciding when and how to respond in a way that generates trust instead of conflict.

Why Reactivity Doesn't Work in Stepfamilies

When stepparents are disrespected or ignored, they may feel a tremendous need to correct, explain, or defend themselves. You may wish to make a point, stand up for yourself, or ensure your feelings are heard. This makes sense; however, being reactive generally makes things worse, not better, especially if you don't have a strong bond with the child yet. Kids may already feel like they're being watched all the time. A stepparent's angry or emotional reaction typically validates their suspicions that this new adult is a threat, not a friend. And when these things happen repeatedly, even minor conflicts can cause lasting damage. Staying calm sends a different message. It shows that you're not here to control people or fight for power; you're here to help the system that is already in place. That quiet confidence generates trust, slowly but surely.

The Strength of Neutral Answers

Being neutral doesn't mean not getting involved; it means not getting caught up in the drama. It's the ability to see without taking in, to recognize without acting. Try answers like:

- "I get what you're saying." I'll let your parent take care of things.
- "I'm not going to talk about this right now."
- "Let's talk about that later when everyone is calmer."
- "I'm not going to do that." "Let's take a break."

These brief, unambiguous sentences keep the energy in check. They don't make you angry. They don't push back. They just let you know that you're standing your ground and not letting yourself get caught up in emotional upheaval. Neutral reactions are significant because they give people time to cool down, allowing them time to think and facilitating better conversations to come. You're not cutting off communication; you're bringing it back to a healthier pace.

A Leadership Move to Keep Your Peace

It may seem like you're not doing anything when you step away from a heated moment, yet it's one of the most active ways to lead. You may learn how to control your emotions, and how well you do it sets the tone for the whole house. In many stepfamilies, children are already feeling overwhelmed by all the changes. When you choose peace over power, you become someone they can trust, rather than someone they need to fight. Maintaining calmness is beneficial for your mental health because it keeps you grounded. It keeps your energy from being sapped by fights that aren't yours to win. It helps you stay in your job as a helpful adult, not a punisher or enforcer. You don't have to fight to make your point. You don't have to yell to be heard. And you don't have to feel what everyone else in the house is feeling. Your steady, neutral, and emotionally mature presence is frequently more powerful than any correction or order. When things get crazy, your calmness is the quiet strength that helps the whole family get back on track. In the following section, we'll discuss how to set boundaries without feeling guilty and how such subtle limitations can help keep you emotionally healthy and your most essential connections safe.

Protecting the Relationship by Saying Less

In stepfamilies, things often become tense because of what people say, rather than what they do. Words mean a great deal, especially when trust is still new and relationships are just beginning to blossom. Even if you mean well, your words can come out wrong if you talk too fast, correct too often, or explain too much. The things you say don't make
you a good stepparent. It stems from your ability to stay calm, focused, and emotionally open. One of the best ways to protect yourself in this job is to learn to say less. This isn't because your voice doesn't matter; it's because your peace issues more. When you say less, it doesn't mean you have to keep your thoughts to yourself. It is deciding when and how to communicate them so that your words bring people together instead of causing problems.

How Speaking Less Often Makes People Trust You More

When a child doesn't know what you're doing, too many directions, corrections, or even comments can feel like they're getting in the way. Even if you speak kindly, giving the same information over and over can seem domineering or overpowering. The more that happens, the more likely it is that the child will emotionally pull away. Kids need time to get to know you and how they feel about you. That process is slowed down by constant feedback, especially when it sounds like parenting. You give them that room by talking less and watching more. You let the connection evolve at its speed, without any pressure or expectations. When utilized appropriately, silence can be a bridge. It says to the child, "I'm here." I'm not trying to boss you around. And I'm not going to force my way into your life.

Letting the Parent Take Charge

If you want to protect your relationship with your stepchild, one of the best things you can do is allow their original parent to speak for the family when there is a problem or a need for correction. Instead of becoming involved, step aside and let the parent take charge of the conversation, enforce the rules, or deal with the behavior. At first, this may seem unusual, especially if you're accustomed to handling things directly. But it gets clearer over time. The youngster knows who their mum or dad is. You are still a helpful presence, not a competing authority. That dynamic makes things less confusing and less emotionally resistant. Discuss your worry with your partner in private if you need to. Let them spread the word. It has a better chance of being heard and a much lower chance of hurting your relationship with the youngster.

Fighting the Need to Explain Everything

It's normal to want to express your point of view, especially when circumstances are tight. Often, too much explanation makes things worse. Kids might not pay attention. Your partner can feel like they have too much to do. You can find yourself saying the exact words over and over again without anything changing. Instead, say short, calm things like:

- "You and your parent should talk about that."
- "I'm going to back off from this."
- "Let's take a break and come back to this later."

These words retain your distance and stop the energy in the room from getting too high. They are transparent, polite, and safe for your feelings. You don't have to explain everything you do or feel. Your job is not to persuade, but to stay anchored. And sometimes, a few words mean more than a lengthy explanation ever could. In a blended family, relationships are fragile. One nasty word or too much information at the wrong time can create walls that take months or years to break down. You exhibit maturity, knowledge, and respect for the emotional process going on around you when you choose when to talk and when to be quiet. Not talking as much isn't a sign of weakness. It's a plan. It gives relationships space to breathe, emotions time to calm, and trust time to blossom on its own.

CHAPTER 7
Power of Presence Without Pressure
How to show love without doing too much.

Being There Is Enough

Love and work can become intertwined in stepfamily relationships. You could feel like you have to show that you're there by doing things like cooking meals, giving rides, helping with homework, or being there for them when they're upset. You can go too far in your efforts to gain respect, connection, or approval. But in truth, your presence means much more than your productivity. Being there for someone, both physically and emotionally, without pushing, fixing, or controlling them, is one of the most effective ways to build trust in a blended family. When combined with consistency and respect, presence quietly establishes the groundwork for a long-term connection. You don't have to "do it all" to fit in. The more you strive to earn your place by working hard all the time, the more likely you are to lose your serenity. Sometimes, the best thing to do is just to be there, calm, grounded, and emotionally open.

Why Doing Less Makes You More Connected

Children in stepfamilies often undergo numerous changes simultaneously. In this emotional state, what they usually need most is not someone else telling them what to do, but someone who is always there for them without putting any pressure on them. Trying too hard can sometimes push people away. Kids could think that constant effort means they want to be close. They can feel like they owe you something in return, or they might fight back to protect their feelings. The relationship becomes softer when you stop thinking about what you can give and start thinking about how you can just be. You stop trying to control the relationship and let it happen on its own.

This Is What Presence Without Pressure Looks Like

You don't have to be in the spotlight to play an important part. Some of the most critical times come from being calm and steady. Here are some examples of how presence without pressure shows up in everyday life:

- Being close by during a family activity without pressing communication.
- Recognizing a child's anger without giving them quick fixes.
- Helping without pushing if they say no.
- Staying calm when other people are upset.
- Being open but still respecting their emotional

space.

These little things you do or don't do say a lot: "I'm here, and I'm not trying to change you or ask you for anything."

Letting the Relationship Grow on Its Own

It takes time for everyone in a stepfamily to get along. You might not connect right away—or even after months. Some kids take a long time to warm up. It's acceptable if some children never get very close to you. The idea isn't to be close right away; it's to have a harmonious relationship built on mutual respect. Let the connection grow at its speed. The more you let go of attempting to control it, the more likely it is to expand. You can't compel someone to trust you, but you can help them trust you by just being there for them and staying stable through all seasons.

In many cases, the most important connections in stepfamilies aren't made with big gestures; they're formed by being there for one another for years. You don't have to do chores, emotional work, or be involved all the time to show your worth in the home. You are not being judged. You don't have to be more, accomplish more, or fix everything. You're already making a difference just by being there with kindness, patience, and a willingness to be there without any pressure. Don't let stress get in the way of your love. Don't let how much you do define your function; let how well you hold space do that. And believe that just being there—calm, polite, and dependable—is more than enough.

Stop Forcing Connection

One of the hardest things about being in a stepfamily is wanting to connect with a child who doesn't seem to want to communicate with you. You could try everything, such as cooking their favorite dishes, attending events, helping them out, or having fun. Even though you try your best, the child is still distant, guarded, or even angry. This emotional distance can seem like being turned down. It's hard not to feel bad about it. But here's the fact that every stepparent has to know: connection can't be forced. It must happen in its own time and in its way. And a lot of the time, that means stopping far before anything happens. Letting go of the impulse to connect doesn't imply you're giving up. It shows you care about the other person's feelings and are keeping your peace at the same time.

Why Trying Too Hard Doesn't Work

The more you strive to make things closer, the more likely they are to go wrong. Children in blended homes often face feelings of sadness, bewilderment, and divided loyalties. They may struggle to emotionally connect with someone new, especially if they perceive the bond as a threat to their relationship with their other parent or a betrayal of the past. It can be challenging to connect with someone, even when you're being nice. People may think that what you mean by 'warmth' is pressure. What you believe is love might be a duty to them. The more you try, the more they may pull away, making things worse, not better.

Making Distance Safe for Emotions

Interestingly, the best approach to creating trust is not to close the gap, but to stop chasing it. Kids start to let their guard down when they don't think you expect anything from them. When people don't have to feel anything when you're around, it's a safe place to relax. That's when real connection can start, quietly and on their terms. This doesn't mean not paying attention to the child. It is being there for someone without being too much. It involves being nice, showing up on time, and being okay with whatever amount of interaction happens spontaneously. You could:

- Smile at them and let them come to you.
- Help without expecting anything in return.
- Please include children in plans, but don't force them to go.

These simple things help alleviate stress and make it possible for trust to grow steadily in an emotional space.

Letting Go of the Timeline

One of the most frustrating aspects for stepparents is not knowing when, or if, the connection will strengthen. You could want to seek evidence of acceptance, monitor growth, or compare your bond to the one your partner has with the child. But connection isn't a list of things to do. It can't be planned or measured. Some relationships change in just a few months. Some take a long time. And sometimes, a strong bond may never form at all. That doesn't imply you didn't do well. It means you took into account the child's needs, pace, and ability. It makes things tense when you try too hard to connect. You don't build trust by doing things well; you create it by being consistent, patient, and emotionally secure. The best thing you can do is stop trying to make the relationship happen and let it unfold naturally. You don't have to prove your value by forcing proximity. You show it by being calm, respectful, and willing to meet the child where they are, not where you want them to be.

Gentle, Quiet Influence

People generally applaud strong leaders and apparent authority, so the idea of subtle, quiet influence may seem too understated to matter. However, in the context of stepfamily life, this is often the best approach. You are not here to lead by being strict or demanding control. You don't gain more power by forcing people to do what you want. Instead, you gain more power by being consistent, respectful, and emotionally stable. Over time, stepparents who lead softly gain trust. There is no power struggle, no need to be heard over others, and no need to show who is in charge. Instead, it's a consistent presence that you can count on—a nonjudgmental adult who shows you how to act calmly and healthily and allows the relationship to grow on its terms.

You Don't Need Power to Have Influence

People often think that you have to be in charge of a child to change their behavior. But trustworthiness, not control, is what gives you power over others. Kids are more likely to do what someone they trust tells them to do than what someone they don't trust tells them to do.

You don't have to tell people what to do or correct their behavior to guide them. What you do, like how you treat people, how you deal with disagreement, and how you take care of yourself, often says the most about you. When a stepchild watches you stay calm under pressure or politely step back when things get tense, you are showing them how to be emotionally mature in ways that will last a long time. That kind of influence might not be seen. However, with time, those moments become the building blocks of respect.

The Power of Subtlety

Being quiet doesn't equal being passive. It means choosing your moments on purpose. You don't have to rush to fix every problem. You don't butt into talks that don't need your involvement. Instead, you are watching, listening, and only being there when it is wanted. You might not be the loudest person in the room, but you are the one who responds thoughtfully instead of reacting impulsively. You are the one who stays calm throughout disputes, respects others' limits, and makes people feel comfortable by being consistent. Subtle influence is substantial since it doesn't require a response. It asks for one. And those invites, when given without pressure, frequently lead to deeper, more meaningful relationships over time.

Letting Your Actions Speak for Themselves

There will be times when you wish to explain what you do, make your job more straightforward, or get credit for your work. That's normal. But with a little push, you stop worrying about how others see you and start thinking about how you act. Think about this:

- Do I do what I say I'll do, but not promise too much?
- Do I treat everyone in the house the same way?
- Do I respect my own and others' limits?

Just being there may change the mood of a room. When you move with purpose, communicate carefully, and avoid pointless arguments, you set an emotional tone that people start to copy. That's authentic leadership, even if it doesn't appear to be. You don't have to push your way into a child's heart to be important. You don't need to have power, titles, or control to be a constant, guiding presence in their lives. It's not about power; it's about being there. And your capacity to stay calm, respectful, and open to feelings has a significantly greater impact than any regulations or lectures could ever have. Ultimately, the quiet ones often have the most significant impact. Not because they pushed, but because they were kind and allowed the connection to evolve at its own pace.

Mary Dixon

Let the Relationship Grow Naturally

There is sometimes an underlying expectation to "make it work" in stepfamily living. You may want to speed up the bonding process, or fix what was broken before you arrived. People don't always put pressure on you; sometimes it comes from yourself. You want peace. You wish to connect. You want everyone to feel like they are part of a family. However, relationships, especially those that matter, don't grow when they're under stress. They grow via time, space, and respect for one another. As a stepparent, one of the best things you can do for yourself and your stepchild is to let go of the idea that you have to be close right away or even regularly. You make room for sincerity to come out when you let the relationship flourish on its own. You give trust time to grow by not putting any pressure on it or setting deadlines.

The Issue with Making a Bond

Even if you mean well, forcing a connection might cause emotional stress. Children in blended homes are already accustomed to loss, change, and shifting relationships. It can be too much to anticipate a perfect relationship with a stepparent, and it can also seem unjust. If a child thinks you're trying too hard, they may resist. They might pull back, act out, or put some space between them and their feelings. It's not because you're doing something wrong; it's because your emotions are moving at a different speed than theirs. You show respect for their readiness by standing back. You make it clear that you don't want to replace someone, push a connection, or rush something very personal. You are there for them when they are ready, not when you are.

Trust Grows in the Gaps

People can connect in many ways, beyond just talking about their feelings or doing things together. In quiet moments, such as when you're simply walking by someone, doing the same thing every day, or not saying anything meaningful at all, it often grows. A youngster might not talk to you right away, but they see how you handle stress, how you treat their parent, and how you give them space. You can build trust by not pushing them, showing up without a plan, and letting them pick how fast to engage. This type of relationship may not be clear or dramatic. But it stays the same. And that consistency is what makes it strong over time.

Letting Go of the Perfect

There are differences between every stepfamily. The best relationships are the ones that take into account everyone's personality, comfort level, and emotional needs. Stop thinking about what your role should look like in an ideal way. A strong relationship between a stepchild and a stepparent doesn't have to be like a biological bond. It just has to be true. It needs to be based on limits, kindness, and a sense of room to breathe. Your goal is not to be perfect. It's calm. And sometimes, the quietest relationships are the most serene ones. They are without any pressure or need to do anything. One of the most important things you can do is to let the connection develop naturally. It keeps you calm and allows your stepchild to come to you when they want to. That's when real connection starts, not because it was forced, but because it was permitted. You don't have to chase after things to show how much you mean to them. You don't have to speed up the timeline to feel safe. Just keep coming, being yourself, and making room. It could take time to find the link you want, but it will be stronger because you didn't rush it.

CHAPTER 8
Boundaries Aren't Barriers They're Lifelines

You don't need permission to protect your peace.

How to Set Boundaries Without Guilt

Guilt is one of the primary reasons stepparents hesitate to impose limits. You can be afraid that saying "no" makes you seem cold, aloof, or unhelpful. You may worry about letting your partner down or seeming like you don't care about the family. However, the truth is that boundaries are what keep you engaged without becoming burned out. Setting limits does not mean saying no. It's not a refusal to care. It's a method of saying:

- "This is how I stay healthy, present, and available."
- This is how I keep what's essential safe without losing myself in the process.

Find out what makes you tired first.
- Is it hard to deal with the emotional weight of dealing with sibling issues?
- Is it the physical tiredness of always cleaning, planning meals, or dropping things off?
- Is it hard on your mind to feel like you have to "parent" in a capacity that isn't clear?

After identifying those areas, create a list of what you want to keep doing and what you need to let go of. After that, explain that limit openly and gently. No need for an explanation. Just the truth. You don't have to explain things in details when you set boundaries with confidence. When you realize you're not leaving the family, but rather "choosing a sustainable way to stay part of it," the guilt starts to go away.

Boundaries with Kids, Partner, and Self

Every connection in your home may need a different kind of boundary. You don't need to use the same method for everyone. Instead, think of your boundaries as flexible tools designed to meet the needs, history, and constraints you bring to each relationship.

With Kids

Kids could push your buttons, ignore your cues, or treat you as the default adult without even realizing it. But it's not your job to take care of someone else's kids' feelings or plans. You can say:

- "That's not my job; ask your parent."
- "I'll be in the room, but I don't want to talk about this."
- "I care about you, but I need some space right now."

These aren't penalties. They gently remind you that you're there but not in charge of taking care of them.

With Your Partner

Setting limits with your partner can be pretty hard. If your partner relies on you too much to co-parent, prepare, or take care of logistics, you need to reset your expectations:

- "I want to help you, but I can't do your job as a parent for you."
- "Let's split up the work so that neither of us gets too stressed."
- "I'll let you take the lead on the things that aren't mine."

Your spouse might not know how much you're carrying until you step back. Setting limits helps the partnership get back on track.

With Yourself

The limits you set for yourself may be the most significant ones.

- Are you keeping track of your energy?
- Are you letting yourself take a break when you need to?

- Are you putting boundaries on how much emotional work you can do? Ask:
- Is this anything I need to fix?
- Am I doing this because I'm scared or because I have to?
- What do I need right now to feel peaceful and stable?

If you say "no" to overextension, you are saying "yes" to long-term peace. Setting limits on yourself is how you stay true to your principles and what you can do.

"No" Is a Complete Sentence

In a blended family, there will be times when you want to say "yes," even if it's not the right thing for you. The simple act of saying "no" is a skill that has to be practiced. It can mean agreeing to do something, mediating an argument, or showing up for something you're not emotionally ready for. You don't have to explain your decisions in great detail. You don't have to vow to "make it up" later every time you say no. You can say:

- "No, I can't do that."
- "No, that's not something I can do."
- "No, thank you."

These answers are good enough. They come from self-respect, not defiance. If you always say no and then explain why or apologize, it makes it seem like you need to protect your boundaries. You don't. You increase your confidence and set a good example for others every time you say "no" politely and clearly.

Modeling Emotional Maturity

One of the best things you can give to a stepfamily is emotional stability. You don't have to be the one who punishes people, fixes problems, or keeps things together. However, you can demonstrate to others what it means to have healthy boundaries, speak calmly, and manage your emotions effectively. When kids watch you calmly walk away from a fight, respect your own needs, or not take the bait in a disagreement, you teach them something important: peace doesn't need control; it requires intention. This kind of modelling is very crucial for kids who are going through a lot of fighting with their other parent or who are having trouble with their biological parents' emotions. You aren't here to repair it, but you can offer a new way of being without saying a word. Here are some examples of emotional maturity in action:

- Responding instead of reacting when things get tense.
- Saying what you need without blaming anyone.
- Setting limits without feeling bad or angry.
- Being responsible for your energy, not how others act.

You become a calming presence in the home as you live by these values. Not because you make people follow the rules, but because you show balance, clarity, and self- respect.

It's not selfish to have boundaries; they're essential. They help you keep in touch without taking over your life. They help you care without getting angry. And they allow other people, including your partner, your kids, and even yourself, to grow within healthy, respectful boundaries.

People often don't understand, value, or know what your job as a stepparent is. That's why you need to define it yourself. Not by controlling or overdoing things, but by setting calm, clear limits that protect your tranquilly and make it clear what you can do. You don't have to work for your rest. You don't have to tell others what you can't do. You have to honor them and trust that you're making room for a real, enduring connection.

Mary Dixon

CHAPTER 9

You Matter Too Reclaiming Your Identity

You're more than your role — you're a whole person.

Mary Dixon

What Did You Love Before This?

Before you had to deal with school schedules, stress, and discreetly supporting your spouse behind the scenes, you were a person with unique hobbies and an inner world all your own. You might have written, painted, or danced before. You might have had creative projects, weekend rituals, or big aspirations. Perhaps your days used to be full of music, books, nature, or unexpected adventures. No matter what it was, you had parts of yourself that had nothing to do with your family duties. When life gets busy, it's easy to forget about those parts. You might try to fill the holes by giving more of yourself, especially in a blended family where there may not be a clear structure and your role may not be clear. However, devoting all your time without getting anything back might leave you feeling drained and, in the end, cause you to lose touch with who you are. Remembering who you were before the family needed you is the first step in reclaiming your identity. You don't have to travel back in time or take up all of your previous hobbies. But you do need to reconnect with the part of yourself that felt entire, fulfilled, and expressive, outside of your relationships.

Think about this:
- What made me feel alive before this part of my life? What was mine that I was looking forward to?
- What have I quit doing because I thought I didn't have time?

Your replies will guide you back.

Creating Space for You Again

The next stage is to make room for that version of yourself to come back now that you've thought about who you used to be. This isn't about changing everything in your life all at once. It's about making tiny, meaningful choices that respect your needs and give you back your sense of personal space. Making room for yourself could look like:

- Taking 30 minutes per day for a personal routine, such as writing in a journal, reading, or walking.
- Setting aside time without technology to reconnect with your body and mind.
- Reconnecting with old acquaintances, mentors, or creative partners.
- Signing up for a class or event in your neighborhood that has nothing to do with your family.

Even a short period of rest can help you get back on track. Most importantly, let yourself prioritize these times without feeling guilty about it. You can say, "This is for me," and keep that time safe from anyone else. Your family will be better off with a version of you that is stable and happy, not constantly tired.

The Danger of Losing Yourself

When your role in the family becomes the only thing that defines you, something inside you starts to diminish. You may feel valuable, but you no longer feel complete. You work, but you don't do well. You help others, yet you feel like you don't exist in your own life. Many stepparents go through this insidious loss of self without even realizing it at first. Here are some signs that you might be losing touch with who you are:

- You struggle to answer questions about what you like or want to do. You feel bad that no one asks how you're doing.
- The effectiveness of the house's operation has a direct impact on how you feel. When you're alone, you feel uneasy—not because you're lonely, but because you don't know what to do with that space.

The longer this goes on, the harder it is to get back to being yourself. That's why it's essential to notice it early and take small, steady steps to regain your freedom. Your worth doesn't derive from what you do. It comes from who you are, what you do, and how well you can be someone other than what people need from you.

Self-Care Isn't Selfish

We learn that prioritizing yourself is sometimes seen as selfish, especially when you are a caregiver. Resting is often seen as a sign of laziness. Let's be clear: taking care of yourself is not selfish. It shows that you value yourself. It's not about pampering yourself or going to the spa (though those are nice too). Self-care that is real goes deeper. It's the act of always putting your health first, even when no one else is asking you to, even when no one else is looking.

What authentic self-care might look like:
- Saying no to one more thing to do when your body needs a break.
- Not feeling bad about needing time to yourself.
- Paying for therapy, coaching, or personal growth.
- Saying no to family obligations that you didn't agree to take on.
- Trusting your gut, especially when it goes against what other people think.

You don't have to say sorry for taking care of yourself. It's imperative, though. You can't give from an empty cup, and your worth isn't based on how much you give up. Taking better care of yourself also shows your family something important: that emotional wellness is essential, boundaries are crucial, and individuality is worth protecting.

Conclusion: You Are First and Foremost Yourself

Being a stepparent might make you feel like you have to take care of someone else's world all the time. But you're more than just a part of the family. You are not only a partner to someone. You're not just a sidekick. You are a whole person. You are layered, creative, complicated, and entire, even if no one else says so today. You can take up space. You can defend your peace. You can want things, have interests, and live your life without worrying about what other people need. Reclaiming your identity doesn't mean moving away; it means coming back to yourself. And from that position, you'll be there for your life, your relationship, and your family in a way that is authentic, joyous, and lasts.

Mary Dixon

CHAPTER 10:

Talk to Your Partner Not Their Kids

All conflict resolution starts behind closed doors.

The "Private Before Public" Rule

If a child does something that concerns you, crosses a line, or makes the house messy, your first instinct could be to fix it right away. But in a blended family, your reaction can mean more than you think and can make things worse without you even realizing it. The "Private Before Public" rule is a key part of Nacho Parenting. This implies that you and your partner should talk about any problems you have with your stepchild first, not in front of the kid, and not right away.

Why is this so important?

Because someone with emotional authority is often the most effective person to administer punishment and behavioral advice, in most cases, that is the biological parent. When a stepparent speaks out in public, it can seem rude, reactive, or harsh, even if they are being honest and their concerns are genuine. It's not your job to fix things right away. Your job is to tell the person who should address your concerns. That talk should take place quietly, with respect, and away from the kids. Say this in this space:

- "I saw what happened earlier, and I need your

help fixing it."
- "I didn't feel respected at that time." "Can you talk to them about it alone?"
- "I'm stepping back from these kinds of interactions, but I need to know that you'll take care of this."

This structure ensures that everyone is on the same page and prevents fights or confusion in front of the kids.

What to Say (and Not Say)

When Something Happens

It's easy to want to deal with something disagreeable straight away, such as defiance, contempt, or disobedience. But when a stepparent directly corrects a child, they typically become defensive. You might make the problem worse instead of better. That's why what you say is essential, especially when you don't say much. If you have to answer right away, use neutral, boundary-respecting terms that put your partner first:

- "That's something your parent will need to talk to you about."
- "We'll talk about this again later with your mom/dad."
- "I'm leaving this conversation; your parent will take over."

Don't provide lectures or explanations, and avoid trying to argue in real time. It could seem like you're "teaching" at the time, but if you don't have the correct foundation, your words might not be understood and could even hurt the relationship you're trying to develop. Later, when you and your partner are alone and quiet, tell them what you're worried about:

- "It felt like he was ignoring me when he rolled his eyes." Please talk to him about it.
- "She didn't do what we agreed to do." Can you help strengthen that line?

You and your partner will respect each other more if you keep these talks private and to the point. This will also keep the kids from getting upset.

You're Not a Mediator

Stepparents often have to keep the peace. You might be the one trying to make things right, communicate between your spouse and their child, or prevent a fight from escalating. It's an instinct, especially if you want peace in your household. But here's the problem: you're not in charge of those relationships. When you put yourself between your spouse and their child, you take on emotional work that isn't yours, and you make it such that both sides may start to depend on you more than they should. Stop feeling like you have to mediate. Let your partner handle their relationship with their child. You are not the one who fixes things. You are there to help, not to speak on behalf of others. Initially, this change may be challenging to cope with. You might be afraid that things will get worse if you back off. However, most of the time, the reverse is true. When you don't get in the way of the parent-child relationship, it can flourish, and things become clearer. Emotional responsibility is starting to come back to where it belongs. Don't jump in with solutions if there is a conflict. Instead, change direction:

- "I believe this is something you and your

child should work out."
- "I'm here for you if you need me, but I'm not the one to deal with this."
- "I trust you to handle it your way."

This helps you keep your emotional bandwidth and set healthy limits.

Making Teamwork Feel Like Teamwork

One person doing everything doesn't make a strong stepfamily. It's based on shared leadership, open communication, and faith that everyone is doing their job well. It's time to talk about it if your partner doesn't know how much you're carrying or how much emotional control you've displayed. Not out of anger, but out of truth. Say:

- "I want to help you without taking on the role of parent."
- "When problems come up with your kids, I need you to take charge."
- "Let's check in often so we're on the same page and I don't get angry."

What real teamwork looks like in stepfamilies:
- Your partner is responsible for discipline and redirection.
- You're talking about your worries in private, not in front of the kids.
- Agreed on limits, expectations, and how to talk to each other.
- A clear idea of when you'll step in and when

you'll step back.

You don't have to parent together. However, you need to communicate with each other like teammates. You're not asking your partner to make everything better. You're asking them to pay attention. To guide where it counts. And to realize that pulling back isn't the same as checking out; it's a choice that protects the family's mental health.

Your voice matters. You are important. But in the complicated realm of stepfamily relationships, what you say is just as essential as how and when you say it. Talking to your partner instead of their child demonstrates that you are wise, respectful, and emotionally mature. It gives the biological parent room to be a parent while you stay in your supportive, conscious role. You don't have to respond to everything right away. You don't have to protect your spot or settle other people's fights. You don't gain power by controlling others; you earn it by being clear and transparent. Not conflict, but restraint. From private talks that keep the peace in public. You show trust when you talk to your partner first. You set the mood. And over time, that quiet leadership changes the whole situation.

Mary Dixon

CHAPTER 11:
Protect Your Relationship First

Your partnership is the foundation of the family.

Mary Dixon

Don't Let Parenting Stress Kill Romance

When you and your partner are both busy with family life, romance can feel like a long-lost memory. People discuss topics such as meal plans, choreography rotations, or strategies for managing children's behavior. There are many things to do at night, and tiredness often takes the place of closeness. But here's the truth: your relationship needs more than leftovers. There is more to romance than flowers and date nights. When you're stressed out, you start to see your partner more as a co-manager than as a love partner. If this change isn't stopped, it can slowly break down closeness. That's why it's essential to fight for moments of warmth, even when things are messy. Write notes. Look your partner in the eye. Tell a private joke. Hold on to each other for a few seconds longer than usual. These small actions remind you both that your link is more than just the family you're helping; it's also the reason you're forming that family in the first place.

Create Rituals for Reconnection

If you live in a busy mixed family, you'll never be able to reconnect if you wait for the "perfect time." That's why planned rituals are essential. They are like anchors that remind you both that your relationship is worth keeping, no matter how hectic life gets. Rituals don't have to be long or complicated. They have to be significant and consistent. Here are several examples:

- A daily check-in for 15 minutes with no phones, just being there.
- A weekend coffee date where you talk about things other than parenthood.
- A night once a month just for the two of you, with no screens or planning, just reconnecting.
- Send short messages throughout the day to express gratitude, show appreciation, or make someone smile.

These little things help you get closer to each other emotionally. They show that your relationship is essential to you, not just something you think about later. Over time, these moments accumulate into a sense of emotional safety—a reminder that you still have each other, no matter what happens in the house.

Avoid "Kid First, Partner Last" Syndrome

It's easy to get into the habit of always putting the kids first. They need things right away. They are noisy. And when you have a blended family, you could feel even more pressure to "get it right" as you deal with complicated relationships. But when the partnership is always pushed to the back, everything starts to go wrong. Putting your partner last not only hurts your relationship, but it also makes things unstable at home. Kids can tell when the people in their lives aren't connected. The family environment appears to be less safe and less stable. This doesn't imply you don't care about what your kids need. It means you stop acting like your relationship is optional. No, it's not. The emotional base is what holds the whole family together. To make room for your partner, you might need to:

- Putting your partner's point of view ahead of the kids' happiness when you disagree.
- Saying "no" to non-urgent parenting responsibilities so you can spend time together.
- Letting your spouse know that their feelings, needs, and presence matter—not just as a co-

parent, but as your person.

Kids feel safer when they perceive that the adults in the house love each other and are strong. There is no limit to how much love you can give. You don't have to end one connection to keep another safe. A healthy love relationship makes the whole family stronger.

Boundaries Around the Relationship Itself

You need to set limits on your relationship, just as you do with your kids, work, and emotional energy. Without them, outside influences can take over your connection. To keep your relationship safe, you might want to:

- Setting rules about when you talk about parenting, especially when you both have free time.
- Not letting the kids know about certain aspects of your relationship, regardless of their age.
- Not letting stress with your child affect how you treat each other.
- Agreeing on times when you both stop being parents and reconnect as people.

It also implies not letting anger build up without saying anything. You need room to deal with your anger, feel heard, and change your expectations with kindness, not competitiveness. Set a goal together to keep your relationship safe, like a garden. The roots become deeper even with short, inadequate care. You don't have to keep your relationship going out of duty.

It's something to feed because it matters, and when it grows, everything else starts to fall into place. There are levels to blended families. But your partnership is at the heart of it all. If you don't take care of the foundation, it can break, and the whole house will seem unstable.

Mary Dixon

CHAPTER 12:
You're Not Cold — You're Clear

Stepping back doesn't mean stepping away.

Letting Go of the Guilt

Guilt is one of the hardest things for stepparents to deal with. You could feel bad for not "doing more." For making limits. For saying no. For not getting involved when things get worse. For leaving behind things that don't help you. That shame doesn't come from failing; it usually comes from taking on too much responsibility. You probably think that love means working hard. That caring is giving without end. To maintain peace, you must deal with disorder. But you were never supposed to fix someone else's family problems. You don't have to fix things, control them, or always make things work. Your role is to love from a place of strength, you are not giving up. Guilt is a sign, not a fact. When it comes up, ask yourself:

- Is this guilt based on something I did wrong, or is it based on a social norm that I'm questioning?
- Would I feel bad if I were guarding my peace in a different situation?
- Who gains when I feel awful for doing what's good for me?

The truth is that guilt often precedes improvement. It's a

sign that you're breaking old habits. Please don't mistake it for a cause to stay stagnant.

Mary Dixon

Why Doing Less Is Sometimes More Loving

It may seem strange, but "doing less can often be the most loving thing you can do." This is especially true in stepfamily life, where roles are complicated and feelings can run high. Taking a step back can help you set healthier boundaries, build more honest relationships, and feel more connected in the long run. This is why less is more:

- If you don't step in right away, the biological parent can completely own their involvement.
- When you stop doing too much, other people have to get involved.
- You give your emotions space to breathe when you don't overcorrect or constantly monitor them.
- You show how to control your emotions by not reacting.

You're not disengaging when you do less; you're giving others the power to step up. You are choosing to be there intentionally, rather than always being busy. By setting limits, you are expressing respect for the relationship between parent and child and demonstrating trust in the system you have established. How much you take in doesn't show how much you love someone. It demonstrates your ability to remain calm, transparent, and emotionally open without micromanaging or overstepping.

Embracing Peace Over Performance

There is often subtle pressure to excel in blended families. You might think you have to prove your affection, explain why you belong, or "earn" your place in the family by always being helpful, available, and agreeable. But the more you act, the less connected you feel to who you are. You're not being yourself; you're being an image of what you think other people want you to be. Letting go of the urge to perform is the first step towards a peaceful stepfamily existence. This means:

- Not judging your work against that of the biological parent. Not pushing connections that aren't ready.
- Not agreeing solely to avoid a fight.
- Not always showing your worth by giving up things for others.

Your worth was never based on how much you do. It depends on how well you align with your reality. You will find peace when you stop attempting to control how others see things. When you understand that being there quietly, respectfully, and honestly has more of an effect than any performance ever could.

Loving Without Losing Yourself

There is an unwritten understanding in many caregiving situations, especially as a stepparent, that love requires being fully involved. To be a good stepparent, you should always be there for the family, adapt to their needs, and set aside your demands for the sake of unity. But love that makes you lose who you are isn't love; it's depletion. To love people well, you first have to love yourself enough to stay whole. That includes keeping your hobbies, routines, friends, and dreams alive. It means not giving up your voice to make other people feel better. It is being emotionally open without being emotionally overwhelmed. You can love someone a lot and still need space. You can be present and still say no. You can help someone and still keep your boundaries. Healthy love does not mean merging; it means connecting in a way that lets both people stay who they are. Think about this:

- Am I being myself in this family, or am I trying to be someone they will like?
- What aspects of me have I quieted down for the sake of peace?
- What would it be like to bring more of myself back into this space?

When you stop trying to fit into someone else's mold, the love you offer becomes more real, and the relationships you have with other people become stronger.

By choosing clarity above control, peace over doing well. Boundaries are better than burnout. These aren't signals that you're detached; they're signs that you have a lot of emotional wisdom. You aren't cold since you won't go too far. You're not distant because you don't want to discipline. You aren't selfish because you take care of your energy. You are clear about your ideals, your role, and your restrictions. And that is what makes a blended family stable in the long run. Taking a step back doesn't mean quitting. It's stepping into a kind of love that's more mindful, long-lasting, and grounded in truth. One that respects you and your family. One that encourages people to take up their duties completely. One that earns respect over time, without anger.

And most importantly, one that creates room for you—your peace, your happiness, your identity, and your future. This isn't only a way to raise kids. It is a way of life. And you have the right to live it with freedom, respect, and grace.

CONCLUSION:

Loving Smart, Living Peacefully

At some point in every step-parenting journey, you realize that love alone isn't enough. This isn't because your heart isn't enormous; it's because your energy isn't limitless. You've put a lot of effort into this family. You've tried to be there, to solve things, to fit in, and to make peace. And even though your efforts were reasonable, they might have left you feeling empty. It's time to quit giving without thinking and start giving wisely. That involves respecting your emotional limits, setting clear boundaries, and understanding that you don't have to contribute more than your fair share in this family to be important. Smart love isn't about proving how valuable you are; it's about forming connections that energize you instead of draining you. You may adore this family and still keep yourself safe. You can care a lot and not lose yourself. You can help your spouse without being their kids' parent. You can care for someone without feeling like you have to worry about how they think, act, or what happens.

Taking a step back doesn't mean quitting. It's about staying alive. It's the realisation that your well-being is essential and that maintaining your emotional peace is what will help you be present, calm, clear, and confident in yourself. It's picking a new way of living that isn't based on guilt or reacting to things, but on being grounded and intentional. Choosing serenity above performance gives you power. Silence is powerful. There is a lot of love in just being there, not as a fixer, but as a steady, respectful presence. Nacho Parenting doesn't cut you off from your family; it helps you reconnect with yourself. You are not alone on this path. Many stepparents face the same hidden burden, the same uncertainties about their role, and the same fatigue. But what makes you different now is this: you've learnt how to stay in the story without becoming lost in it.

This new you, with stronger limits, softer expectations, and better self-awareness, is not less loving. It's more even. It can take a lot. It's smart. And most importantly, it will last.

As you go on, remember this: You can be there and be safe. You can choose tranquilly over making other people happy. And you can decide what your function is on your terms. You have already contributed enough. Now, give clearly. Be sensible about love. Be at peace. And trust that from this place of strength, you'll keep building connections based on respect, not resentment, and connection, not obligation. This isn't the end of your story as a parent. It's the start of one where you matter, too.

www.ingramcontent.com/pod-product-compliance
Lightning Source LLC
Chambersburg PA
CBHW071240070526
44583CB00017B/2260